Supporting Maths

FOR AGES 9–10

Andrew Brodie

Introduction

Supporting Maths is aimed at all those who work with children who have been identified as needing 'additional' or 'different' support in mathematics. It can be used by anyone working with children who fall into this category, whether you are a teacher, classroom assistant or parent.

Typically the nine to ten year-old children for whom the book is intended will be working at the levels expected of Year 3 or Year 4 children or they may simply need extra help in tackling the level of work appropriate for Year 5. Their difficulties may be short term, and overcome with extra practice and support on a one-to-one or small group basis, or they may be long term, where such support enables them to make progress but at a level behind their peer group. The *Record and Review* sheet on page 5 is ideal for keeping track of the targets you set and the progress made by each child.

The 2006 Framework for Teaching Mathematics specifies seven strands of learning:

- Strand 1   *Using and applying mathematics*
- Strand 2   *Counting and understanding number*
- Strand 3   *Knowing and using number facts*
- Strand 4   *Calculating*
- Strand 5   *Understanding shape*
- Strand 6   *Measuring*
- Strand 7   *Handling data*

This book addresses all seven strands, drawing on the objectives from Year 3, Year 4 and Year 5. Particular emphasis is placed on understanding number, using number facts and calculating with these. The *Individual record sheet* on page 3 shows the aspects of the seven strands that can be assessed through using the worksheets and through discussion with the pupil.

In this book we provide activities that can be effectively completed on paper, with the help of an adult. The interaction with the adult gives many opportunities for speaking and listening. Explanation by an adult to a child and vice versa provides a firm foundation for mathematical understanding. To reinforce understanding, many activities should be completed in a practical context e.g. children could compare sizes of real objects; they could perform practical addition by combining two groups of objects; they could use base ten equipment to observe the effect of 'crossing tens boundaries'.

Many activities address the key skills of adding and subtracting. Number lines are provided for practical support and lots of tips and suggestions for approaches that are logical and achievable are outlined in the *Notes for teachers* on each page. Year 5 children will also be extending their knowledge of multiplication tables to cover division facts. In this book we provide practice of all the tables from 2 to 10 and link these to division questions. Children need to see that division is closely related to multiplication and that subtraction is closely related to addition. Several worksheets deal with the processes of doubling and halving of numbers - a useful skill. These skills will be useful for children when making estimations of quantities. And finally, for an 'at a glance guide' to useful facts and figures children can refer to the mini facts on Resource sheet F at the back of this book.

However you decide to use these sheets and in whatever context, it is worth remembering that children generally achieve the greatest success in an atmosphere of support and encouragement. Praise from a caring adult can be the best reward for the children's efforts. The worksheets and activities in this book will provide many opportunities for children to enjoy their successes. (As a visual reminder, children can also complete the *My record sheet* on page 4). The development of a positive attitude and the resulting increase in self-esteem will help them with all of their school work and other areas of school life too.

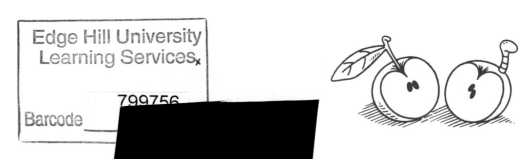

Andrew B...   ...ublishers Ltd. 2007

Individual record sheet

Name:

Worksheet	Contents	Teaching and learning objective	Target achieved	Needs more practice
1-6	Addition and subtraction within 20	Strands 1, 2, 3, 4, 6		
7-12	Addition and subtraction of 2-digit numbers	Strands 1, 2, 3, 4, 6		
13	Subtraction of 2-digit numbers from 100	Strands 1, 2, 3, 4, 6		
14	Subtraction of 2-digits or 3-digits from 200	Strands 1, 2, 3, 4, 6		
15	Subtraction of 2-digits or 3-digits from 500	Strands 1, 2, 3, 4, 6		
16-17	Addition of money	Strands 1, 2, 3, 4, 6		
18-21	Finding change	Strands 1, 2, 3, 4, 6		
22-23	Reading/writing 3-digit and 4-digit numbers	Strands 1, 2		
24	Number sequences	Strands 1, 2, 4		
25-27	Adding multiples of 10, 100, 1000	Strands 1, 2, 3, 4, 6		
28-30	Finding doubles	Strands 1, 3		
31-33	Finding halves	Strands 1, 3		
34	The 2 times table	Strands 1, 3, 4		
35	The 3 times table	Strands 1, 3, 4		
36	The 4 times table	Strands 1, 3, 4		
37	The 5 times table	Strands 1, 3, 4		
38	The 6 times table	Strands 1, 3, 4		
39	The 7 times table	Strands 1, 3, 4		
40	The 8 times table	Strands 1, 3, 4		
41	The 9 times table	Strands 1, 3, 4		
42	The 10 times table	Strands 1, 3, 4		
43-48	Decimals and fractions	Strands 1, 2, 3		
49	Measuring to the nearest millimetre	Strands 1, 6		
50	Perimeters and areas of rectangles	Strands 1, 6		
51	Reading and plotting coordinates	Strands 1, 5		
52-53	Tallying and drawing a bar chart	Strands 1, 7		
Resource sheets A-E	Times tables	Strand 3		
Resource sheet F	Mini facts	Strand 2, 3, 5, 6		

My record sheet

Name: _____   Date of birth: _____

Class: _____   Date: _____

I can...

- select and use suitable equipment and information ☐
- explain decisions, methods and results ☐
- read and write two-digit numbers ☐
- read and write three-digit numbers ☐
- read and write four-digit numbers ☐
- read and write decimals with one place ☐
- read and write decimals with two places ☐
- recognise odd and even numbers ☐
- recall all addition and subtraction facts for numbers to 20 ☐
- add and subtract multiples of 10 ☐
- add a one-digit number to any two-digit number ☐
- add a multiple of 10 to any two-digit number ☐
- add a two-digit number to any two-digit number ☐
- add multiples of 100 ☐
- add multiples of 1000 ☐
- subtract a one-digit number from any two-digit number ☐
- subtract a multiple of 10 from any two-digit number ☐
- subtract a two-digit number from a two-digit number ☐
- subtract any two-digit number from 100 ☐
- subtract any two-digit number from 200 ☐

- subtract any two-digit number from 500 ☐
- add sums of money up to £2 ☐
- add sums of money up to £10 ☐
- find change from 50p ☐
- find change from £1 ☐
- find change from £5 ☐
- find change from £10 ☐
- derive and recall the 2 times table and use it to find divisions ☐
- derive and recall the 3 times table and use it to find divisions ☐
- derive and recall the 4 times table and use it to find divisions ☐
- derive and recall the 5 times table and use it to find divisions ☐
- derive and recall the 6 times table and use it to find divisions ☐
- derive and recall the 7 times table and use it to find divisions ☐
- derive and recall the 8 times table and use it to find divisions ☐
- derive and recall the 9 times table and use it to find divisions ☐
- derive and recall the 10 times table and use it to find divisions ☐
- calculate divisions by using diagrams ☐
- find doubles of numbers from 1 to 10 ☐

- find doubles of multiples of 10 ☐
- find doubles of numbers from 11 to 100 ☐
- find halves of two-digit numbers ☐
- find halves of multiples of 100 ☐
- find halves, quarters and three quarters of shapes ☐
- recognise the role of the denominator in a fraction ☐
- recognise the role of the numerator in a fraction ☐
- multiply any number from 1 to 100 by 10 ☐
- continue number sequences with steps of constant size ☐
- measure lengths using standard units ☐
- identify common 2D shapes in different positions ☐
- sort common 2D shapes, referring to their properties ☐
- measure the perimeters of rectangles on a grid ☐
- find the areas of rectangles on a grid ☐
- use coordinates to describe position ☐
- use tallying to record data ☐
- use a bar chart to record data ☐

Andrew Brodie: Supporting Maths © A & C Black Publishers Ltd. 2007

Record and Review

Name: _____ Date of birth: _____

Teacher: _____ Class: _____

Support assistant: _____

Code of Practice stage: _____ Date targets set: _____

Target

1 _____

2 _____

3 _____

4 _____

Review

Target

1 _____

_____

_____ Target achieved? ☐ Date: _____

2 _____

_____

_____ Target achieved? ☐ Date: _____

3 _____

_____

_____ Target achieved? ☐ Date: _____

4 _____

_____

_____ Target achieved? ☐ Date: _____

worksheet 1

Name: Date:

0 1 2 3 4 5 6 7 8 9 10

How quickly can you answer these questions?

4 + 2 = ☐	7 + 3 = ☐	8 + 2 = ☐
1 + 7 = ☐	4 + 4 = ☐	5 + 3 = ☐
6 + 2 = ☐	3 + 5 = ☐	5 + 4 = ☐
9 + 1 = ☐	5 + 2 = ☐	5 + 5 = ☐
1 + 3 = ☐	8 + 1 = ☐	6 + 3 = ☐
7 + 2 = ☐	4 + 5 = ☐	7 + 2 = ☐

2 + 7 = ☐	2 + 2 = ☐	5 + 2 = ☐
6 + 1 = ☐	4 + 1 = ☐	6 + 3 = ☐
6 + 2 = ☐	4 + 2 = ☐	3 + 7 = ☐
6 + 3 = ☐	4 + 3 = ☐	2 + 8 = ☐
6 + 4 = ☐	4 + 4 = ☐	1 + 4 = ☐
6 + 0 = ☐	4 + 5 = ☐	8 + 3 = ☐

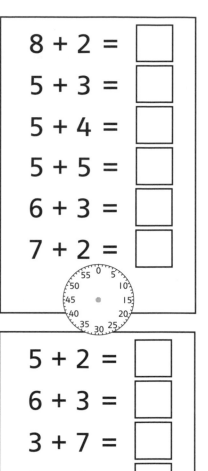

Notes for teachers

Target: Solve one-step problems involving numbers, money or measures, including time; represent the information using numbers or diagrams; identify patterns or relationships involving numbers; describe and explain methods (Strand 1). Read, write and order numbers and position them on a number line (Strand 3). Derive and recall all addition facts for all numbers to at least 10. Add a one-digit number to a one-digit number (Strand 4). Interpret intervals and divisions on partially numbered scales and record readings accurately; calculate time intervals (Strand 6).

Allow the child to practise a few 'warm up' questions on paper before starting the activity. Some children choose to use their fingers but watch carefully how they do this as mistakes often happen when a child counts a particular finger more than once! Some children find the questions easier if they use a pencil to move along the line e.g. starting with the pencil on 4 then moving on 2 to find the answer to the first question. Encourage the child to decide which number to start on e.g. on questions such as 1 + 7 it is quicker to start at the 7 then move on 1. Help the child to time her/himself using a clock or watch with a second hand. To make this easier, encourage the child to start each set of questions when the second hand is on twelve. S/he should then record the number of seconds taken, on the clock face provided. S/he will need to observe carefully where the second hand has reached by the time s/he has completed the set of six questions. This process encourages the child both to observe the small markings on the clock and to work as quickly as possible. Discuss the questions and answers with the pupil. Can s/he see any patterns? Can s/he find the doubles? Which question has an answer that is more than 10? Which questions all have the answer 10?

Name: _____   **Date:** _____

0 1 2 3 4 5 6 7 8 9 10

How quickly can you answer these questions?

9 – 6 = ☐	9 – 8 = ☐	8 – 3 = ☐
7 – 4 = ☐	10 – 5 = ☐	7 – 7 = ☐
6 – 1 = ☐	8 – 4 = ☐	10 – 4 = ☐
8 – 2 = ☐	6 – 6 = ☐	9 – 2 = ☐
7 – 3 = ☐	9 – 3 = ☐	6 – 4 = ☐
4 – 4 = ☐	10 – 9 = ☐	7 – 3 = ☐

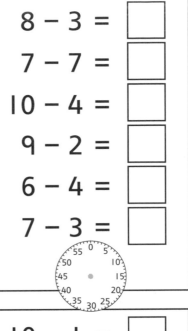

9 – 1 = ☐	8 – 1 = ☐	10 – 1 = ☐
9 – 3 = ☐	8 – 3 = ☐	10 – 8 = ☐
9 – 4 = ☐	8 – 4 = ☐	10 – 4 = ☐
9 – 8 = ☐	8 – 7 = ☐	10 – 3 = ☐
9 – 2 = ☐	8 – 2 = ☐	10 – 7 = ☐
9 – 7 = ☐	8 – 5 = ☐	10 – 5 = ☐

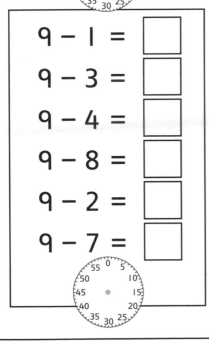

Notes for teachers

Target: Solve one-step problems involving numbers, money or measures, including time; represent the information using numbers or diagrams; identify patterns or relationships involving numbers; describe and explain methods (Strand 1). Read, write and order numbers and position them on a number line (Strand 2). Derive and recall all subtraction facts for all numbers to at least 10 (Strand 3). Subtract a one-digit number from a one-digit or two-digit number (Strand 4). Interpret intervals and divisions on partially numbered scales and record readings accurately; calculate time intervals (Strand 6). Allow the child to practise a few 'warm up' questions on paper before starting the activity. Some children find the questions easier if they use a pencil to move along the line e.g. the pencil could be placed on the 9 then moved back 6 to find the answer to the first question. Point out that 9 – 6 is not the same as 6 – 9 but that the child could start on the 9 and move back 6 or start on the 6 and count on to the 9. In either case s/he is finding the difference between the two numbers. Help the child to time her/himself using a clock or watch with a second hand. To make this easier, encourage the child to start each set of questions when the second hand is on twelve. S/he should then record the number of seconds taken, on the clock face provided. This process encourages the child both to observe the small markings on the clock and to work as quickly as possible. When each set of questions has been answered discuss the answers with the child, encouraging her/him to notice any patterns such as where two questions both produce the same answer.

Name: _____ **Date:** _____

0 1 2 3 4 5 6 7 8 9 10

How quickly can you answer these questions?

$9 - 2 = \square$	$9 + 1 = \square$	$8 - 4 = \square$
$6 + 4 = \square$	$10 - 2 = \square$	$7 - 6 = \square$
$6 - 3 = \square$	$6 + 3 = \square$	$6 + 2 = \square$
$8 + 2 = \square$	$7 - 5 = \square$	$5 + 4 = \square$
$4 - 3 = \square$	$4 + 3 = \square$	$9 - 4 = \square$
$5 - 5 = \square$	$5 + 2 = \square$	$10 - 4 = \square$

$5 + 2 = \square$	$8 + 1 = \square$	$10 - 6 = \square$
$9 - 3 = \square$	$8 - 1 = \square$	$6 + 4 = \square$
$8 - 5 = \square$	$6 + 4 = \square$	$4 + 6 = \square$
$1 + 7 = \square$	$6 - 4 = \square$	$10 - 3 = \square$
$3 + 3 = \square$	$5 - 2 = \square$	$7 + 3 = \square$
$10 - 5 = \square$	$5 + 2 = \square$	$3 + 7 = \square$

Notes for teachers

Target: Solve one-step problems involving numbers, money or measures, including time; represent the information using numbers or diagrams; identify patterns or relationships involving numbers; describe and explain methods (Strand 1). Read, write and order numbers and position them on a number line (Strand 2). Derive and recall all addition and subtraction facts for all numbers to at least 10 (Strand 3). Add a one-digit number to a one-digit number; subtract a one-digit number from a one-digit or two-digit number (Strand 4). Interpret intervals and divisions on partially numbered scales and record readings accurately; calculate time intervals (Strand 6).

After completing worksheets 1 and 2, this worksheet provides revision of addition and subtraction within 10. Encourage the child to look carefully at the sign in each number sentence. Many children make mistakes simply because they have not done so. After each set of questions discuss the answers with the child, encouraging her/him to notice any patterns such as where two questions both produce the same answer. The final set of questions contains two groups of questions that have strong connections. Discuss these links with the child.

Andrew Brodie: Supporting Maths © A & C Black Publishers Ltd. 2007

worksheet 4

0 1 2 3 4 5 6 7 8 9 10 11 12 13 14 15 16 17 18 19 20

How quickly can you answer these questions?

$6 + 2 =$ ☐	$1 + 3 =$ ☐	$3 + 2 =$ ☐
$16 + 2 =$ ☐	$11 + 3 =$ ☐	$13 + 2 =$ ☐
$7 + 2 =$ ☐	$4 + 5 =$ ☐	$2 + 7 =$ ☐
$17 + 2 =$ ☐	$14 + 5 =$ ☐	$12 + 7 =$ ☐
$12 + 3 =$ ☐	$8 + 1 =$ ☐	$6 + 3 =$ ☐
$2 + 3 =$ ☐	$18 + 1 =$ ☐	$16 + 3 =$ ☐

$5 + 2 =$ ☐	$2 + 2 =$ ☐	$5 + 1 =$ ☐
$15 + 2 =$ ☐	$12 + 2 =$ ☐	$15 + 3 =$ ☐
$6 + 4 =$ ☐	$4 + 3 =$ ☐	$3 + 4 =$ ☐
$16 + 4 =$ ☐	$14 + 3 =$ ☐	$13 + 4 =$ ☐
$4 + 4 =$ ☐	$5 + 5 =$ ☐	$6 + 2 =$ ☐
$14 + 4 =$ ☐	$15 + 5 =$ ☐	$16 + 2 =$ ☐

Notes for teachers

Target: Solve one-step problems involving numbers, money or measures, including time; represent the information using numbers or diagrams; identify patterns or relationships involving numbers; describe and explain methods (Strand 1). Read, write and order numbers and position them on a number line (Strand 2). Derive and recall all addition facts for each number to twenty (Strand 3). Add a one-digit number to a one-digit or two-digit number (Strand 4). Interpret intervals and divisions on partially numbered scales and record readings accurately; calculate time intervals (Strand 6).

The questions on this sheet provide more practice of mental addition. When each set of questions has been answered discuss the answers with the child, encouraging her/him to notice any patterns, particularly relationships such as those between questions like 7 + 2, 17 + 2, 2 + 7, 12 + 7. Our arrangement of questions has made some of these relationships quite obvious but sometimes a child needs help in noticing the obvious!

Name: **Date:**

0 1 2 3 4 5 6 7 8 9 10 11 12 13 14 15 16 17 18 19 20

How quickly can you answer these questions?

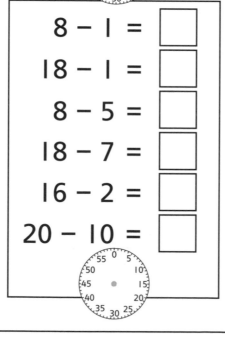

18 – 6 =	9 – 8 =	5 – 3 =
8 – 6 =	19 – 8 =	15 – 3 =
18 – 13 =	8 – 4 =	15 – 13 =
18 – 3 =	18 – 4 =	9 – 2 =
8 – 3 =	18 – 14 =	19 – 2 =
14 – 7 =	18 – 9 =	16 – 8 =

9 – 1 =	8 – 1 =	12 – 7 =
19 – 1 =	18 – 1 =	15 – 8 =
19 – 11 =	8 – 5 =	17 – 4 =
9 – 8 =	18 – 7 =	19 – 3 =
19 – 8 =	16 – 2 =	20 – 7 =
12 – 6 =	20 – 10 =	10 – 5 =

Notes for teachers

Target: Solve one-step problems involving numbers, money or measures, including time; represent the information using numbers or diagrams; identify patterns or relationships involving numbers; describe and explain methods (Strand 1). Read, write and order numbers and position them on a number line. Derive and recall all subtraction facts for each number to twenty (Strand 3). Subtract a one-digit or two-digit number from a two-digit number (Strand 4). Interpret intervals and divisions on partially numbered scales and record readings accurately; calculate time intervals (Strand 6).

Allow the child to practise a few 'warm up' questions before starting the activity. Help the child to time her/himself using a clock or watch with a second hand. When each set of questions has been answered discuss the answers with the child, encouraging her/him to notice any patterns e.g. the answer to the last question in each set has the same value as the number being subtracted. Help the child to understand that 'fourteen subtract seven equals seven because two sevens are fourteen'. Encourage the child to decide whether to solve each question by 'jumping back' or by 'counting on' e.g. with the question 18 – 6 the child can start at 18 on the number line and 'jump back' 6 to arrive at the answer 12 or start at the 6 and 'count on' 12 places to 18. Ask the child which of these methods would be quicker for this question. Compare this question to the question 18 – 13. Is it quicker to jump back 13 from 18 or to count on from 13 to 18?

Name: _____ **Date:** _____

worksheet 6

Addition and Subtraction within 20

0 1 2 3 4 5 6 7 8 9 10 11 12 13 14 15 16 17 18 19 20

12 + 6 = ☐	19 – 8 = ☐	15 – 3 = ☐
5 + 7 = ☐	4 + 6 = ☐	7 + 8 = ☐
16 – 7 = ☐	12 – 9 = ☐	9 – 7 = ☐
8 + 3 = ☐	7 + 6 = ☐	9 + 6 = ☐
16 – 9 = ☐	20 – 5 = ☐	14 + 3 = ☐
13 – 6 = ☐	20 – 9 = ☐	17 – 9 = ☐

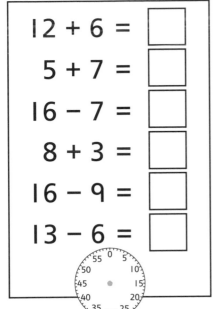 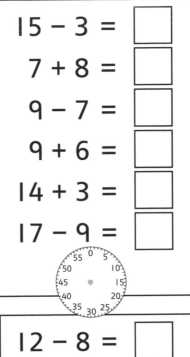

12 + 4 = ☐	11 – 7 = ☐	12 – 8 = ☐
20 – 13 = ☐	7 + 7 = ☐	6 + 9 = ☐
12 – 8 = ☐	15 – 9 = ☐	17 – 8 = ☐
14 + 5 = ☐	12 + 5 = ☐	9 + 7 = ☐
15 – 8 = ☐	16 + 4 = ☐	20 – 1 = ☐
12 + 6 = ☐	20 – 17 = ☐	8 + 4 = ☐

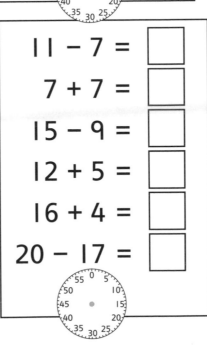

Notes for teachers
Target: Solve one-step problems involving numbers, money or measures, including time; represent the information using numbers or diagrams; identify patterns or relationships involving numbers; describe and explain methods (Strand 1). Read, write and order numbers and position them on a number line (Strand 2). Derive and recall all subtraction facts for each number to twenty (Strand 3). Add a one-digit number to a one-digit or two-digit number; subtract a one-digit or two-digit number from a two-digit number (Strand 4). Interpret intervals and divisions on partially numbered scales and record readings accurately; calculate time intervals (Strand 6).
After completing worksheets 4 and 5 this worksheet provides revision of addition and subtraction within 20. Encourage the child to look carefully at the sign in each number sentence. Many children make mistakes simply because they have not done so. When each set of questions has been answered discuss the answers with the child, helping her/him to notice any patterns. We have deliberately not included any obvious patterns on this worksheet to encourage the child to use their increasing knowledge and skills to answer each question individually. Repeated practice can help children gain confidence in their number work.

Name: _____ **Date:** _____

0   10   20   30   40   50   60   70   80   90   100

How quickly can you answer these questions?

36 + 7 = ☐	48 + 7 = ☐	25 + 8 = ☐
49 + 2 = ☐	69 + 5 = ☐	59 + 2 = ☐
23 + 5 = ☐	84 + 6 = ☐	62 + 7 = ☐
67 + 2 = ☐	35 + 8 = ☐	88 + 7 = ☐
82 + 9 = ☐	28 + 5 = ☐	26 + 3 = ☐
59 + 3 = ☐	77 + 7 = ☐	34 + 3 = ☐

65 + 9 = ☐	79 + 2 = ☐	79 + 1 = ☐
41 + 9 = ☐	72 + 9 = ☐	98 + 1 = ☐
56 + 4 = ☐	68 + 3 = ☐	68 + 4 = ☐
28 + 4 = ☐	24 + 9 = ☐	23 + 8 = ☐
37 + 7 = ☐	37 + 5 = ☐	56 + 6 = ☐
91 + 9 = ☐	45 + 5 = ☐	96 + 7 = ☐

Notes for teachers

Target: Solve one-step problems involving numbers, money or measures, including time; represent the information using numbers or diagrams; identify patterns or relationships involving numbers; describe and explain methods (Strand 1). Read, write and order numbers and position them on a number line (Strand 2). Use knowledge of addition and subtraction facts (Strand 3). Add a one-digit number to a two-digit number (Strand 4). Interpret intervals and divisions on partially numbered scales and record readings accurately; calculate time intervals (Strand 6).

The questions on this sheet provide more practice of mental addition with the aid of a number line. Allow the child to practise a few 'warm up' questions on paper before starting the activity. If you find that the child does not use the number line for the addition process take the opportunity to discuss the number line with her/him. Ask her/him to show you where some of the 'start numbers' would appear on the number line provided. Can s/he judge where 36 should be, for example? Can s/he judge where the answer to 36 + 7 should be? Understanding numbers in relation to the number line will help the child answer questions without a number line.

Name: _____ **Date:** _____

Use number lines to help you answer these questions.

0 10 20 30 40 50 60 70 80 90 100

42 + 23 = ☐
58 + 39 = ☐

68 + 19 = ☐
18 + 18 = ☐

27 + 24 = ☐
49 + 39 = ☐

0 10 20 30 40 50 60 70 80 90 100

56 + 27 = ☐
28 + 29 = ☐

47 + 38 = ☐
62 + 34 = ☐

73 + 17 = ☐
66 + 34 = ☐

0 10 20 30 40 50 60 70 80 90 100

82 + 17 = ☐
35 + 25 = ☐

29 + 18 = ☐
43 + 16 = ☐

57 + 26 = ☐
40 + 33 = ☐

Notes for teachers

Target: Solve one-step problems involving numbers, money or measures, including time; represent the information using numbers or diagrams; identify patterns or relationships involving numbers; describe and explain methods (Strand 1). Read, write and order numbers and position them on a number line (Strand 2). Use knowledge of addition and subtraction facts (Strand 3). Add a two-digit number to a two-digit number. Interpret intervals and divisions on partially numbered scales and record readings accurately; calculate time intervals (Strand 6).

These questions are not timed as the child will need to think very carefully to complete them. Help the child to identify the position of the 'start number' on a number line e.g. for the first question ask her/him to show you where the 42 would be, then to add on 23. Show her/him that the adding on can be completed in two parts: s/he could jump on 20 to reach 62 then count on the extra 3 to reach the answer 65. Or, s/he could count on the 3 units first to reach 45 then jump on 20 to reach 65. The answer to the last question is 100, which could lead to an extension activity where the child has to find other pairs of numbers that add up to 100. Repeated practice is an excellent way of building children's confidence in their number work.

Name: _____   **Date:** _____

0   10   20   30   40   50   60   70   80   90   100

How quickly can you answer these questions?

50 – 6 =	☐
90 – 6 =	☐
40 – 6 =	☐
70 – 3 =	☐
50 – 7 =	☐
30 – 1 =	☐

90 – 8 =	☐
60 – 2 =	☐
80 – 6 =	☐
30 – 4 =	☐
70 – 7 =	☐
40 – 9 =	☐

70 – 4 =	☐
80 – 8 =	☐
50 – 6 =	☐
90 – 7 =	☐
30 – 2 =	☐
40 – 5 =	☐

70 – 1 =	☐
30 – 6 =	☐
90 – 5 =	☐
50 – 8 =	☐
40 – 3 =	☐
80 – 5 =	☐

70 – 9 =	☐
90 – 1 =	☐
60 – 8 =	☐
40 – 4 =	☐
50 – 7 =	☐
20 – 3 =	☐

80 – 4 =	☐
20 – 8 =	☐
60 – 4 =	☐
90 – 3 =	☐
100 – 7 =	☐
70 – 8 =	☐

Notes for teachers

Target: Solve one-step problems involving numbers, money or measures, including time; represent the information using numbers or diagrams; identify patterns or relationships involving numbers; describe and explain methods (Strand 1). Read, write and order numbers nand position them on a number line (Strand 2). Use knowledge of addition and subtraction facts (Strand 3). Subtract a one-digit or two-digit number from a two-digit number (Strand 4). Interpret intervals and divisions on partially numbered scales and record readings accurately; calculate time intervals (Strand 6).

Before starting these questions you may like to remind the child of the number bonds for 10. You could ask the child to complete a list of subtractions from ten i.e. 10 – 0 = 10, 10 – 1 = 9, 10 – 2 = 8, etc. S/he could keep this list to refer to when working out the answers on this sheet. Allow the child to practise a few 'warm up' questions before starting the activity, providing help if necessary.

Name: _____   **Date:** _____

```
0    10   20   30   40   50   60   70   80   90   100
```

How quickly can you answer these questions?

48 – 6 = ☐	99 – 8 = ☐	78 – 3 = ☐
31 – 6 = ☐	41 – 5 = ☐	81 – 3 = ☐
23 – 7 = ☐	83 – 6 = ☐	44 – 6 = ☐
91 – 3 = ☐	22 – 4 = ☐	65 – 9 = ☐
64 – 7 = ☐	74 – 7 = ☐	19 – 2 = ☐
52 – 8 = ☐	31 – 9 = ☐	16 – 8 = ☐

38 – 4 = ☐	68 – 9 = ☐	52 – 7 = ☐
81 – 7 = ☐	74 – 5 = ☐	25 – 8 = ☐
92 – 5 = ☐	33 – 5 = ☐	61 – 4 = ☐
43 – 4 = ☐	93 – 6 = ☐	99 – 3 = ☐
51 – 8 = ☐	84 – 7 = ☐	45 – 7 = ☐
72 – 6 = ☐	42 – 10 = ☐	75 – 9 = ☐

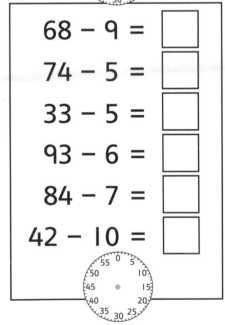

Notes for teachers
Target: Solve one-step problems involving numbers, money or measures, including time; represent the information using numbers or diagrams; identify patterns or relationships involving numbers; describe and explain methods (Strand 1). Read, write and order numbers and position them on a number line (Strand 2). Use knowledge of addition and subtraction facts (Strand 3). Subtract a one-digit or two-digit number from a two-digit number (Strand 4). Interpret intervals and divisions on partially numbered scales and record readings accurately; calculate time intervals (Strand 6).
Allow the child to practise a few warm up questions before starting the activity, providing help if necessary. Encourage her/him to complete these subtractions by counting back. Where the counting back crosses the tens boundary, you could encourage the child to count back to the nearest multiple of ten, then to see how much further s/he needs to count back using knowledge of subtractions from multiples of ten. Once again, s/he could use the list of subtractions from ten as clues to help her/him with these questions.

Name: _____   **Date:** _____

Use number lines to help you answer these questions.

0   10   20   30   40   50   60   70   80   90   100

66 – 28 = ☐	32 – 13 = ☐	62 – 38 = ☐
81 – 36 = ☐	55 – 27 = ☐	75 – 45 = ☐

0   10   20   30   40   50   60   70   80   90   100

74 – 19 = ☐	92 – 24 = ☐	83 – 58 = ☐
37 – 21 = ☐	78 – 23 = ☐	65 – 29 = ☐

0   10   20   30   40   50   60   70   80   90   100

46 – 19 = ☐	62 – 34 = ☐	85 – 37 = ☐
94 – 66 = ☐	54 – 16 = ☐	96 – 57 = ☐

Notes for teachers

Target: Solve one-step problems involving numbers, money or measures, including time; represent the information using numbers or diagrams; identify patterns or relationships involving numbers; describe and explain methods (Strand 1). Read, write and order numbers and position them on a number line (Strand 2). Use knowledge of addition and subtraction facts. Subtract a two-digit number from a two-digit number (Strand 4). Interpret intervals and divisions on partially numbered scales and record readings accurately (Strand 6).

Demonstrate the first few questions to the child using the following technique for counting on:
(i) Starting with the lower number, draw a curved arrow on the number line to the next multiple of ten and ask the child how far you have jumped (e.g., on the first question draw an arrow from the position of 28 to the number 30); (ii) from this multiple of ten jump in tens and draw an arrow to the multiple of ten below the higher number and ask the child how far you have jumped e.g. on the first question draw an arrow from the 30 to the 60; (iii) draw an arrow making the final jump and ask the child how far you have jumped this time e.g. on the first question draw an arrow from the 60 to the 66; (iv) ask the child how far you have jumped altogether. You may like to encourage the child to draw several more number lines to answer the rest of the questions.

Name: _____ **Date:** _____

worksheet
12

Use number lines to help you answer these questions.

0 10 20 30 40 50 60 70 80 90 100

| 77 – 38 = ☐ | 43 – 34 = ☐ | 61 – 39 = ☐ |
| 81 – 67 = ☐ | 51 – 28 = ☐ | 84 – 45 = ☐ |

0 10 20 30 40 50 60 70 80 90 100

| 64 – 32 = ☐ | 78 – 56 = ☐ | 90 – 68 = ☐ |
| 52 – 36 = ☐ | 52 – 27 = ☐ | 78 – 34 = ☐ |

0 10 20 30 40 50 60 70 80 90 100

| 41 – 27 = ☐ | 95 – 78 = ☐ | 80 – 37 = ☐ |
| 33 – 10 = ☐ | 61 – 42 = ☐ | 73 – 29 = ☐ |

Notes for teachers

Target: Solve one-step problems involving numbers, money or measures, including time; represent the information using numbers or diagrams; identify patterns or relationships involving numbers; describe and explain methods (Strand 1). Read, write and order numbers and position them on a number line (Strand 2). Use knowledge of addition and subtraction facts (Strand 3). Subtract a two-digit number from a two-digit number (Strand 4). Interpret intervals and divisions on partially numbered scales and record readings accurately (Strand 6).

This worksheet provides further practice of the important skill of finding the difference using a number line. Demonstrate the first few questions to the child using the following technique for counting on:

(i) starting with the lower number, draw a curved arrow on the number line to the next multiple of ten and ask the child how far you have jumped e.g. on the first question draw an arrow from the position of 38 to the number 40; (ii) from this multiple of ten jump in tens and draw an arrow to the multiple of ten below the higher number and ask the child how far you have jumped e.g. on the first question draw an arrow from the 40 to the 70;

(iii) draw an arrow making the final jump and ask the child how far you have jumped this time e.g. on the first question draw an arrow from the 70 to the 77; (iv) ask the child how far you have jumped altogether.

You may like to encourage the child to draw several more number lines ready to answer the rest of the questions.

Andrew Brodie: Supporting Maths © A & C Black Publishers Ltd. 2007

Name: _____   Date: _____

Use number lines to help you answer these questions.

0   10   20   30   40   50   60   70   80   90   100

100 − 63 = ☐	
100 − 89 = ☐	

100 − 13 = ☐	
100 − 39 = ☐	

100 − 25 = ☐	
100 − 54 = ☐	

0   10   20   30   40   50   60   70   80   90   100

100 − 94 = ☐	
100 − 38 = ☐	

100 − 43 = ☐	
100 − 46 = ☐	

100 − 58 = ☐	
100 − 23 = ☐	

0   10   20   30   40   50   60   70   80   90   100

100 − 87 = ☐	
100 − 72 = ☐	

100 − 99 = ☐	
100 − 67 = ☐	

100 − 32 = ☐	
100 − 11 = ☐	

Notes for teachers

Target: Solve one-step problems involving numbers, money or measures, including time; represent the information using numbers or diagrams; identify patterns or relationships involving numbers; describe and explain methods (Strand 1). Read, write and order numbers and position them on a number line (Strand 2). Use knowledge of addition and subtraction facts (Strand 3). Subtract a two-digit number from 100 (Strand 4). Interpret intervals and divisions on partially numbered scales and record readings accurately (Strand 6).

This worksheet provides excellent practice in preparation for finding change when working with money. Many children make mistakes when subtracting from 100 e.g. on the first question, they are likely to subtract 60 from 100 to successfully reach 40 but then to subtract the 3 from 10 to reach 7 and to produce the answer 47 instead of 37. This type of error is actually made by children who are quite competent with number work but who need to take a closer look at the process. The number line is ideal for this.

Demonstrate the first few questions to the child using the following technique:
(i) starting with the lower number, draw a curved arrow on the number line to the next multiple of ten and ask the child how far you have jumped e.g. on the first question draw an arrow from the position of 63 to the number 70; (ii) from this multiple of ten jump in tens and draw an arrow to the 100 e.g. on the first question draw an arrow from the 70 to the 100; (iii) ask the child how far you have jumped altogether.

Name: _____   **Date:** _____

worksheet
14

You may decide to use number lines to help you answer these questions.

0 10 20 30 40 50 60 70 80 90 100 110 120 130 140 150 160 170 180 190 200

200 – 150 = ☐	200 – 113 = ☐
200 – 73 = ☐	200 – 22 = ☐
200 – 132 = ☐	200 – 151 = ☐

0 10 20 30 40 50 60 70 80 90 100 110 120 130 140 150 160 170 180 190 200

200 – 102 = ☐	200 – 175 = ☐
200 – 98 = ☐	200 – 25 = ☐
200 – 167 = ☐	200 – 148 = ☐

0 10 20 30 40 50 60 70 80 90 100 110 120 130 140 150 160 170 180 190 200

200 – 87 = ☐	200 – 125 = ☐
200 – 120 = ☐	200 – 64 = ☐
200 – 44 = ☐	200 – 149 = ☐

Notes for teachers
Target: Solve one-step problems involving numbers, money or measures, including time; represent the information using numbers or diagrams; identify patterns or relationships involving numbers; describe and explain methods (Strand 1). Read, write and order numbers and position them on a number line (Strand 2). Use knowledge of addition and subtraction facts (Strand 3). Subtract a two-digit number from 100 (Strand 4). Interpret intervals and divisions on partially numbered scales and record readings accurately (Strand 6).
This worksheet provides further practice in preparation for finding change when working with money. These subtractions also help children to develop further their mental maths skills as they begin to know whether their answers are reasonable and become more capable of making sensible estimations. Allow them to find the answer to each question by jumping back from 200 or by jumping on from the smaller number. They do not have to use the number lines but if they make any errors you could discuss the questions with them using the number lines as visual aids.

Andrew Brodie: Supporting Maths © A & C Black Publishers Ltd. 2007

Name: _____ **Date:** _____

You may decide to use number lines to help you answer these questions.

0   50   100   150   200   250   300   350   400   450   500

$500 - 499 =$ ☐ $500 - 92 =$ ☐

$500 - 259 =$ ☐ $500 - 112 =$ ☐

$500 - 342 =$ ☐ $500 - 289 =$ ☐

$500 - 121 =$ ☐ $500 - 4 =$ ☐

$500 - 68 =$ ☐ $500 - 388 =$ ☐

$500 - 301 =$ ☐ $500 - 219 =$ ☐

$500 - 250 =$ ☐ $500 - 325 =$ ☐

$500 - 251 =$ ☐ $500 - 73 =$ ☐

$500 - 487 =$ ☐ $500 - 260 =$ ☐

Notes for teachers

Target: Solve one-step problems involving numbers, money or measures, including time; represent the information using numbers or diagrams; identify patterns or relationships involving numbers; describe and explain methods (Strand 1). Read, write and order numbers and position them on a number line (Strand 2). Use knowledge of addition and subtraction facts (Strand 3). Subtract a two-digit number from 100 (Strand 4). Interpret intervals and divisions on partially numbered scales and record readings accurately (Strand 6).

This worksheet provides excellent practice in preparation for finding change from £5. Watch out for the mistake that children often make with this type of question. On the first question, for example, some children are likely to subtract the 400 to find 100 then to subtract 99 from 100 to find 1 but to add this 1 to 100 and to give the answer 101! The number line should overcome this.

Name: _____   **Date:** _____

£0   £0.50   £1   £1.50   £2

Find the total amounts of money.

63p + 47p = ☐   19p + 35p = ☐

27p + 36p = ☐   51p + 41p = ☐

84p + 32p = ☐   76p + 83p = ☐

17p + 73p = ☐   78p + 56p = ☐

11p + 45p = ☐   57p + 43p = ☐

54p + 28p = ☐   34p + 91p = ☐

31p + 98p = ☐   90p + 54p = ☐

82p + 5p = ☐   45p + 76p = ☐

96p + 46p = ☐   4p + 87p = ☐

Notes for teachers
Target: Solve one-step problems involving numbers, money or measures, including time; represent the information using numbers or diagrams; identify patterns or relationships involving numbers; describe and explain methods (Strand 1). Read, write and order numbers and position them on a number line (Strand 2). Use knowledge of addition and subtraction facts (Strand 3). Add mentally pairs of two-digit whole numbers (Strand 4). Interpret intervals and divisions on partially numbered scales and record readings accurately (Strand 6).
Help the child to use the number line to answer these questions. Make sure that s/he understands that the number line is marked in pounds and that '£0.50' means the same amount as '50p'. Before starting the questions you could ask the child to show you the positions of particular amounts of money on the number line e.g. 'Show me where 63 pence would be on the number line.' The child may need some help in writing down the answers where the total amount exceeds £1.

Name: _____   **Date:** _____

£0   £1   £2   £3   £4   £5   £6   £7   £8   £9   £10

Find the total amounts of money.

£1.42 + £1.85 = ☐   £5.08 + £2.96 = ☐

£3.56 + £2.99 = ☐   £7.84 + £1.32 = ☐

£2.75 + £4.87 = ☐   £2.56 + £3.94 = ☐

£1.50 + £2.09 = ☐   £1.97 + £6.43 = ☐

£5.38 + £3.45 = ☐   £5.04 + £1.69 = ☐

£2.17 + £3.49 = ☐   £3.86 + £2.11 = ☐

£2.94 + £6.01 = ☐   £5.97 + £2.93 = ☐

£4.81 + £1.67 = ☐   £8.54 + £0.73 = ☐

£2.37 + £7.62 = ☐   £2.95 + £3.06 = ☐

Notes for teachers

Target: Solve one-step problems involving numbers, money or measures, including time; represent the information using numbers or diagrams; identify patterns or relationships involving numbers; describe and explain methods (Strand 1). Read, write and order numbers and position them on a number line (Strand 2). Use knowledge of addition and subtraction facts (Strand 3). Refine and use efficient written methods to add and subtract money (Strand 4). Interpret intervals and divisions on partially numbered scales and record readings accurately (Strand 6).

There are several ways that the child can approach these questions. Help her/him to answer them, using the number line if necessary. You could suggest that s/he combines the whole pounds first, then adds the pence, making sure that if there is more than 100 pence s/he realises that s/he has more than another whole pound.

Name: _____ **Date:** _____

0   10p   20p   30p   40p   50p

Find the change from 50p.

50p − 26p = ☐   50p − 45p = ☐

50p − 35p = ☐   50p − 14p = ☐

50p − 41p = ☐   50p − 39p = ☐

50p − 48p = ☐   50p − 12p = ☐

50p − 7p = ☐   50p − 25p = ☐

50p − 29p = ☐   50p − 4p = ☐

50p − 36p = ☐   50p − 40p = ☐

50p − 18p = ☐   50p − 17p = ☐

50p − 3p = ☐   50p − 32p = ☐

Notes for teachers

Target: Solve one-step problems involving numbers, money or measures, including time; represent the information using numbers or diagrams; identify patterns or relationships involving numbers; describe and explain methods (Strand 1). Read, write and order numbers and position them on a number line (Strand 2). Use knowledge of addition and subtraction facts (Strand 3). Refine and use efficient written methods to add and subtract money (Strand 4). Interpret intervals and divisions on partially numbered scales and record readings accurately (Strand 6).

Help the child in answering the questions, using the number line if necessary. The questions can be solved by starting at the 50p then taking away the lower amount to find out how much money is left or by starting at the lower amount of money then counting on to 50p (the traditional shop-keepers' method before the introduction of electronic tills). The child may need some help in judging the position of each value on the number line but this process is a valuable aspect of developing understanding. After the child has completed some of the questions using the number line, you may like to answer some or all of the questions using real coins.

Name: _____

Date: _____

Change from £1

0p   10p   20p   30p   40p   50p   60p   70p   80p   90p   £1

Find the change from £1.

£1 – 53p = ☐   £1 – 93p = ☐

£1 – 87p = ☐   £1 – 58p = ☐

£1 – 1p = ☐   £1 – 6p = ☐

£1 – 62p = ☐   £1 – 68p = ☐

£1 – 24p = ☐   £1 – 10p = ☐

£1 – 75p = ☐   £1 – 66p = ☐

£1 – 50p = ☐   £1 – 83p = ☐

£1 – 71p = ☐   £1 – 97p = ☐

£1 – 89p = ☐   £1 – 46p = ☐

Notes for teachers

Target: Solve one-step problems involving numbers, money or measures, including time; represent the information using numbers or diagrams; identify patterns or relationships involving numbers; describe and explain methods (Strand 1). Read, write and order numbers Nand position them on a number line (Strand 2). Use knowledge of addition and subtraction facts (Strand 3). Refine and use efficient written methods to add and subtract money (Strand 4). Interpret intervals and divisions on partially numbered scales and record readings accurately (Strand 6).

Help the child to answer the questions, using the number line if necessary. The questions can be solved by starting at the £1 then taking away the lower amount to find out how much money is left or by starting at the lower amount of money then counting on to £1. After the child has completed some of the questions using the number line, s/he could answer some or all of the questions using real coins.

          Andrew Brodie: Supporting Maths © A & C Black Publishers Ltd. 2007

Name: _____   **Date:** _____

0   £1   £2   £3   £4   £5

Find the change from £5.

£5 − £1.85 = ☐   £5 − £2.65 = ☐

£5 − £2.99 = ☐   £5 − £4.43 = ☐

£5 − £3.28 = ☐   £5 − £0.85 = ☐

£5 − £1.29 = ☐   £5 − £1.91 = ☐

£5 − £4.73 = ☐   £5 − £3.56 = ☐

£5 − £4.15 = ☐   £5 − £2.06 = ☐

£5 − £4.99 = ☐   £5 − £2.83 = ☐

£5 − £3.74 = ☐   £5 − £4.60 = ☐

£5 − £1.49 = ☐   £5 − £1.77 = ☐

Notes for teachers

Target: Solve one-step problems involving numbers, money or measures, including time; represent the information using numbers or diagrams; identify patterns or relationships involving numbers; describe and explain methods (Strand 1). Read, write and order numbers and position them on a number line (Strand 2). Use knowledge of addition and subtraction facts (Strand 3). Refine and use efficient written methods to add and subtract money (Strand 4). Interpret intervals and divisions on partially numbered scales and record readings accurately (Strand 6).

Help the child to answer the questions, using the number line if necessary. The questions can be solved by starting at the £5 then taking away the lower amount to find out how much money is left or by starting at the lower amount of money then counting on to £5. After the child has completed some of the questions using the number line, s/he could answer some or all of the questions using real coins. You could ask the child to try some of the questions without using any visual aids. Can s/he visualise the process in her/his head?

Name: _____ **Date:** _____

£0   £1   £2   £3   £4   £5   £6   £7   £8   £9   £10

Work with your teacher to answer these questions.

£10 − £3.42 = ☐	£10 − £6.81 = ☐
£10 − £7.74 = ☐	£10 − £1.43 = ☐
£10 − £8.19 = ☐	£10 − £5.08 = ☐

£10 − £9.26 = ☐	£10 − £0.94 = ☐
£10 − £4.37 = ☐	£10 − £3.69 = ☐
£10 − £2.65 = ☐	£10 − £6.24 = ☐

£10 − £4.86 = ☐	£10 − £2.19 = ☐
£10 − £0.17 = ☐	£10 − £7.13 = ☐
£10 − £8.55 = ☐	£10 − £9.72 = ☐

Notes for teachers

Target: Solve one-step problems involving numbers, money or measures, including time; represent the information using numbers or diagrams; identify patterns or relationships involving numbers; describe and explain methods (Strand 1). Read, write and order numbers Nand position them on a number line (Strand 2). Use knowledge of addition and subtraction facts (Strand 3). Refine and use efficient written methods to add and subtract money (Strand 4). Interpret intervals and divisions on partially numbered scales and record readings accurately (Strand 6).

Help the child to answer the questions, using the number line if necessary. The questions can be solved by starting at the £10 then taking away the lower amount to find out how much money is left or by starting at the lower amount of money then counting on to £10. After the child has completed some of the questions using the number line, s/he could answer some or all of the questions using real coins. You could then ask the child to try some of the questions without using any visual aids. Can s/he visualise the process in her/his head?

 Andrew Brodie: Supporting Maths © A & C Black Publishers Ltd. 2007

Name: _____   **Date:** _____

worksheet
22

This number is four hundred and fifty-two:

hundreds	tens	units
4	5	2

Match the numbers. The first one has been done for you.

seven hundred and thirteen ———————————╮ 317

five hundred ╭──────────────────╯ 649

one hundred and ninety-six ╰──────── 713

three hundred and seventeen 196

six hundred and forty-nine 500

nine hundred and sixty-seven 730

seven hundred and thirty 967

Listen to your teacher. Write the numbers.

Notes for teachers

Target: Identify patterns and relationships involving numbers (Strand 1). Read, write and order whole numbers to at least 1000 (Strand 2).

You could cut off these teachers' notes so that the child cannot see the numbers that you are going to dictate to her/him. Ask the child to look carefully at the number 452, explaining that the 4 is in the hundreds column, the 5 is in the tens column and the 2 is in the units column. S/he may need help in reading the word form of the numbers but the purpose of the exercise is to read the numbers in figures correctly, as many children find difficulty in reading numbers beyond 100. When the child is ready, dictate the following numbers to her/him:

169   207   674   913   782   404   367   998   319   550

Watch carefully how the child writes each number and correct any misunderstandings. Numbers such as 207 and 404 often cause difficulty for children and may need to be discussed. You could extend the activity by asking questions such as: 'What is one more than six hundred and ninety-nine?' 'What is one less than eight hundred?'

Andrew Brodie: Supporting Maths © A & C Black Publishers Ltd. 2007

Name: _____   Date: _____

This number is six thousand, three hundred and forty nine:

thousands	hundreds	tens	units
6	3	4	9

Match the numbers. The first one has been done for you.

five thousand, two hundred and twelve   2937

two thousand, nine hundred and thirty-seven   8575

four thousand and three   5121

five thousand, one hundred and twenty-one   5212

nine thousand, six hundred and eight   1001

eight thousand, five hundred and seventy-five   9608

one thousand and one   4003

Listen to your teacher. Write the numbers.

Notes for teachers

Target: Identify patterns and relationships involving numbers (Strand 1). Read, write and order whole numbers to at least 1000 (Strand 2).

You may decide to cut off these teachers' notes so that the child cannot see the numbers that you are going to dictate to her/him. Ask the child to look carefully at the number 6349, explaining that the 6 is in the thousands column, the 3 is in the hundreds column, the 4 is in the tens column and the 9 is in the units column. S/he may need help in reading the word form of the numbers but the purpose of the exercise is to read the numbers in figures correctly as many children have difficulty reading numbers beyond 100. When the child is ready, dictate the following numbers to her/him:

3445   2187   5628   9008   6042   8521   7051   3062   8406   1982

Watch carefully how the child writes each number and correct any misunderstandings. Numbers such as 9008 and 6042 often cause difficulty for children and may need to be discussed. You could extend the activity by asking questions such as: 'What is one more than five thousand, two hundred and ninety-nine?' 'What is one less than ten thousand?'

2　　　　　4　　　　　6　　　　　8　　　　　10

This is called a number sequence: 2, 4, 6, 8, 10…

What is the next number in the sequence? ☐ … and the next number? ☐

Look at the number sequences below. Write two more numbers for each one.

4, 6, 8, 10, 12, ☐ , ☐　　　　7, 10, 13, 16, 19, ☐ , ☐

4, 9, 14, 19, 24, ☐ , ☐　　　　52, 48, 44, 40, 36, ☐ , ☐

6, 14, 22, 30, 38, ☐ , ☐　　　　50, 44, 38, 32, 26, ☐ , ☐

8, 19, 30, 41, 52, ☐ , ☐

Notes for teachers

Target: Solve one-step problems involving numbers, money or measures, including time, choosing and carrying out appropriate calculations; follow a line of enquiry by deciding what information is important; identify patterns or relationships involving numbers; describe and explain methods (Strand 1). Recognise and continue number sequences formed by counting on or back in steps of constant size (Strand 2). Add or subtract mentally combinations of one-digit and two-digit numbers (Strand 4).

Help the child to look carefully at the example sequence, identifying the fact that the numbers are increasing by two and finding the two missing numbers. When the child approaches the questions you could suggest that s/he draws a small arrow between each pair of numbers and labels the arrow with the value that is being added or subtracted

e.g. 4, ₊₂ 6, ₊₂ 8, ₊₂ 10, ₊₂ 12,

Name: _____   **Date:** _____

Work with your teacher to answer these questions. You could draw number lines on a separate piece of paper to help you. The first number line has been drawn for you.

60   70   80   90   100   110   120   130   140   150   160

60 + 80 = ☐   110 + 60 = ☐   180 + 60 = ☐

50 + 60 = ☐   30 + 40 = ☐   60 + 50 = ☐

70 + 20 = ☐   80 + 70 = ☐   80 + 40 = ☐

40 + 80 = ☐   150 + 30 = ☐   110 + 70 = ☐

20 + 90 = ☐   70 + 60 = ☐   90 + 30 = ☐

10 + 50 = ☐   20 + 40 = ☐   30 + 170 = ☐

Now listen to your teacher. Answer the questions.

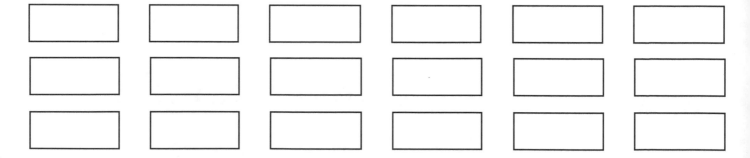

Notes for teachers

Target: Solve one-step problems involving numbers, money or measures, including time; represent the information using numbers or diagrams; identify patterns or relationships involving numbers; describe and explain methods (Strand 1). Read, write and order numbers and position them on a number line (Strand 2). Use knowledge of addition facts to derive sums of pairs of multiples of 10 (Strand 3). Add mentally pairs of two-digit whole numbers (Strand 4). Interpret intervals and divisions on partially numbered scales and record readings accurately (Strand 6).

You may decide to cut off the questions below before asking the child to complete the sheet. Help the child to draw and use number lines to answer the questions printed at the top of the sheet. The first number line is provided. Discuss this one with the child, pointing out that it doesn't start at zero but at 60 instead because that is the first number in the question. S/he can draw her/his own number lines, marked in tens and starting at one of the numbers in the question. If s/he feels confident to answer the questions without number lines this is to be encouraged. Once s/he is competent in these, explain that you are going to read out some questions and that s/he can answer them using number lines if necessary, then dictate some or all of the following questions.

80 + 120 =	50 + 20 =	100 + 190 =	90 + 80 =	120 + 130 =	170 + 140 =
40 + 90 =	90 + 140 =	40 + 170 =	60 + 150 =	150 + 120 =	190 + 220 =
100 + 170 =	150 + 70 =	180 + 40 =	80 + 140 =	180 + 160 =	130 + 180 =

Work with your teacher to answer these questions. You may like to draw number lines on a separate piece of paper to help you. The first number line has been drawn for you.

```
500        600        700        800        900       1000
►|──────────|──────────|──────────|──────────|──────────|──────►
```

$500 + 400 =$ ☐ $900 + 200 =$ ☐ $600 + 700 =$ ☐

$300 + 200 =$ ☐ $600 + 500 =$ ☐ $400 + 600 =$ ☐

$100 + 700 =$ ☐ $400 + 800 =$ ☐ $1300 + 500 =$ ☐

$700 + 600 =$ ☐ $800 + 300 =$ ☐ $700 + 900 =$ ☐

$200 + 400 =$ ☐ $300 + 500 =$ ☐ $1500 + 700 =$ ☐

$500 + 300 =$ ☐ $700 + 800 =$ ☐ $1000 + 400 =$ ☐

Now listen to your teacher. Answer the questions.

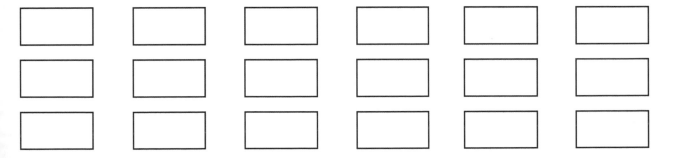

Notes for teachers

Target: Solve one-step problems involving numbers, money or measures, including time; represent the information using numbers or diagrams; identify patterns or relationships involving numbers; describe and explain methods (Strand 1). Read, write and order numbers and position them on a number line (Strand 2). Use knowledge of addition facts to derive sums of pairs of multiples of 100 (Strand 3). Interpret intervals and divisions on partially numbered scales and record readings accurately (Strand 6).

You may decide to cut off the questions below before asking the child to complete the sheet. Help the child to draw and use number lines to answer the questions printed at the top of the sheet. The first number line is provided. Discuss this one with the child, pointing out that it doesn't start at zero but at 500 instead because that is the first number in the question. On a separate piece of paper s/he can draw her/his own number lines, marked in hundreds and starting at one of the numbers in the question. If s/he feels confident to answer the questions without number lines this is to be encouraged. Again, on a separate piece of paper s/he may like to make notes to help her/him answer the questions. Once s/he is competent in these, explain that you are going to read out some questions and that s/he can answer them using number lines if necessary, then dictate some or all of the following questions.

1200 + 300 =	1500 + 800 =	1700 + 1200 =	1200 + 1900 =	900 + 1500 =	2900 + 1600 =
1800 + 600 =	700 + 500 =	1400 + 1400 =	600 + 1800 =	1200 + 2400 =	1800 + 1700 =
500 + 900 =	1100 + 400 =	1500 + 700 =	1300 + 1600 =	1300 + 1900 =	3600 + 2500 =

Name: _____   **Date:** _____

Work with your teacher to answer these questions. You may like to draw number lines on a separate piece of paper to help you. The first number line has been drawn for you.

4000   5000   6000   7000   8000   9000   10000

$4000 + 3000 =$ ☐ $2000 + 7000 =$ ☐

$3000 + 7000 =$ ☐ $3000 + 5000 =$ ☐

$2000 + 5000 =$ ☐ $6000 + 2000 =$ ☐

$1000 + 4000 =$ ☐ $1000 + 6000 =$ ☐

$5000 + 2000 =$ ☐ $4000 + 5000 =$ ☐

$6000 + 3000 =$ ☐ $5000 + 4000 =$ ☐

Now listen to your teacher. Answer the questions.

☐ ☐ ☐ ☐ ☐ ☐

☐ ☐ ☐ ☐ ☐ ☐

☐ ☐ ☐ ☐ ☐ ☐

Notes for teachers

Target: Solve one-step problems involving numbers, money or measures, including time; represent the information using numbers or diagrams; identify patterns or relationships involving numbers; describe and explain methods (Strand 1). Read, write and order numbers and position them on a number line (Strand 2). Use knowledge of addition facts to derive sums of pairs of multiples of 1000 (Strand 3). Interpret intervals and divisions on partially numbered scales and record readings accurately (Strand 6).

You may decide to cut off the questions below before asking the child to complete the sheet. Help the child to draw and use number lines to answer the questions printed at the top of the sheet. The first number line is provided. Discuss this one with the child, pointing out that it doesn't start at zero but at 4000 instead because that is the first number in the question. On a separate piece of paper s/he can draw her/his own number lines, marked in hundreds and starting at one of the numbers in the question. If s/he feels confident to answer the questions without number lines this is to be encouraged. Again, on a separate piece of paper s/he may like to make notes to help her/him answer the questions. Once s/he is competent in these, explain that you are going to read out some questions and that s/he can answer them using number lines if necessary, then dictate some or all of the following questions.

$1000 + 8000 =$	$9000 + 5000 =$	$12000 + 3000 =$	$15000 + 7000 =$	$18000 + 4000 =$	$14000 + 17000 =$
$4000 + 7000 =$	$4000 + 6000 =$	$19000 + 8000 =$	$13000 + 8000 =$	$15000 + 12000 =$	$25000 + 9000 =$
$7000 + 8000 =$	$7000 + 7000 =$	$17000 + 6000 =$	$16000 + 9000 =$	$6000 + 15000 =$	$27000 + 24000 =$

How many wheels are there in this picture?

What number is double thirty? ☐

Now try these questions.

double 50 = ☐   double 70 = ☐   double 40 = ☐

double 100 = ☐   double 80 = ☐   double 30 = ☐

double 150 = ☐   double 60 = ☐   double 20 = ☐

double 140 = ☐   double 90 = ☐   double 230 = ☐

Notes for teachers

Target: Solve one-step problems involving numbers, money or measures, including time; identify patterns or relationships involving numbers; describe and explain methods (Strand 1). Derive and recall multiplication facts; use knowledge of number operations including doubling; identify the doubles of two-digit numbers; use these to calculate doubles of multiples of 10 and 100 (Strand 3).

Before starting this activity check that the child can double one-digit numbers by asking her/him some questions such as 'double three', 'double eight', etc. Then check that s/he can double multiples of ten by asking questions such as 'double thirty', 'double sixty', etc. If needs be, show her/him how to solve these questions using a number line or use the working out space. As a final activity s/he may also like to create a 'ready reckoner' showing the doubles of all the one-digit numbers and of the multiples of 10 to 100. Have spare paper ready for the pupil to use for working out.

What number is double
twenty-three?

Step 1:   Find double 20   double 20 = ☐

Step 2:   Find double 3   double 3 = ☐

Step 3:   Add the two answers together ☐ + ☐ = ☐

Now try these questions.

double 14 = ☐   double 35 = ☐   double 16 = ☐

double 89 = ☐   double 25 = ☐   double 47 = ☐

double 32 = ☐   double 27 = ☐   double 41 = ☐

double 15 = ☐   double 46 = ☐   double 18 = ☐

Notes for teachers

Target: Solve one-step problems involving numbers, money or measures, including time; identify patterns or relationships involving numbers; describe and explain methods (Strand 1). Derive and recall multiplication facts; use knowledge of number operations including doubling; identify the doubles of two-digit numbers (Strand 3).
The child should complete this sheet after completing Worksheet 28. When you think that s/he is ready, help the child work through the example of double 23 then answer the other questions in the same way. Encourage her/him to use the working out space. Watch carefully how the child does the working out, providing help where necessary. Have spare paper ready for the pupil to use for working out.

Name: _____   **Date:** _____

worksheet 30

How many boots do you think there are in this picture?

You can count them if you want to.

Now try these questions.

double 280 = ☐   double 170 = ☐   double 190 = ☐

double 240 = ☐   double 110 = ☐   double 260 = ☐

double 150 = ☐   double 340 = ☐   double 400 = ☐

double 470 = ☐   double 380 = ☐   double 580 = ☐

Notes for teachers

Target: Solve one-step problems involving numbers, money or measures, including time; identify patterns or relationships involving numbers; describe and explain methods (Strand 1). Derive and recall multiplication facts; use knowledge of number operations including doubling; identify the doubles of two-digit numbers; use these to calculate doubles of multiples of 10 and 100 (Strand 3).

The child should complete this worksheet after completing worksheets 28 and 29. When you think that s/he is ready support the child in working through double 280 then in answering the other questions in the same way. Encourage her/him to use the working out space. Watch carefully how the child does the working out, providing help where necessary. Have spare paper ready for the pupil to use for working out.

Andrew Brodie: Supporting Maths © A & C Black Publishers Ltd. 2007   35

Name: _____   Date: _____

What number is half of forty-eight?

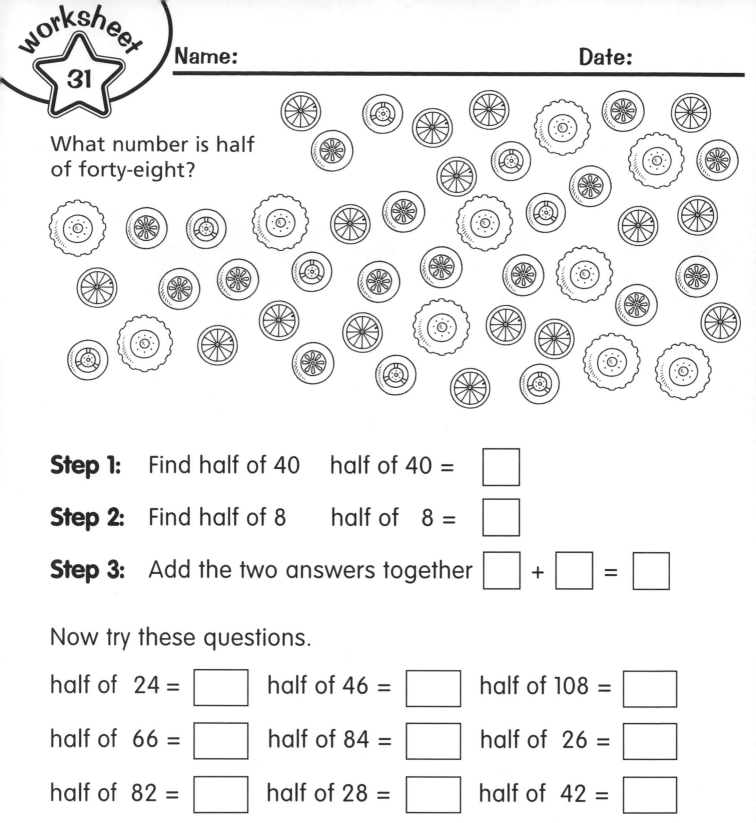

Step 1:   Find half of 40   half of 40 = ☐

Step 2:   Find half of 8   half of 8 = ☐

Step 3:   Add the two answers together ☐ + ☐ = ☐

Now try these questions.

half of 24 = ☐   half of 46 = ☐   half of 108 = ☐

half of 66 = ☐   half of 84 = ☐   half of 26 = ☐

half of 82 = ☐   half of 28 = ☐   half of 42 = ☐

half of 104 = ☐   half of 62 = ☐   half of 112 = ☐

Notes for teachers

Target: Solve one-step problems involving numbers, money or measures, including time; identify patterns or relationships involving numbers; describe and explain methods (Strand 1). Derive and recall multiplication facts and the corresponding division facts; use knowledge of number operations and corresponding inverses, including doubling and halving; identify the doubles of two-digit numbers (Strand 3).

Note that these questions all feature numbers that have an even number in the tens column so that when halving the tens element the answers will be multiples of ten rather than five e.g. half of 80 is 40. On worksheet 32 we feature questions such as 'half of 32' where the child will first need to find half of the 30. Encourage her/him to use the working out space. As an extra activity you may like to return to the example at the top of the page and ask the child to find half of each type of wheel, then to add the results to find the same total as before. Have spare paper ready for the pupil to use for working out.

Name: **Date:**

What number is half
of thirty-two?

Step 1: Find half of 30   half of 30 = ☐

Step 2: Find half of 2   half of 2 = ☐

Step 3: Add the two answers together ☐ + ☐ = ☐

Now try these questions.

half of 10 = ☐   half of 56 = ☐   half of 58 = ☐

half of 90 = ☐   half of 72 = ☐   half of 70 = ☐

half of 96 = ☐   half of 50 = ☐   half of 78 = ☐

half of 30 = ☐   half of 34 = ☐   half of 36 = ☐

Notes for teachers
Target: Solve one-step problems involving numbers, money or measures, including time; identify patterns or relationships involving numbers; describe and explain methods (Strand 1). Derive and recall multiplication facts and the corresponding division facts; use knowledge of number operations and corresponding inverses, including doubling and halving; identify the doubles of two-digit numbers (Strand 3).
Many children find difficulty in halving numbers such as 30 where the tens digit is an odd number. Help the child by suggesting s/he splits the 30 into 20 and 10, then to find half of 20 and half of 10 and to combine the two answers. Encourage her/him to use the working out space. Watch carefully how the child does the working out, providing help where necessary. As an extra activity you may like to return to the example at the top of the page and ask the child to find half the number of each type of vehicle, then to add the results to find the same total as before. Have spare paper ready for the pupil to use for working out.

Name:

Date:

This picture shows
one hundred wheels.

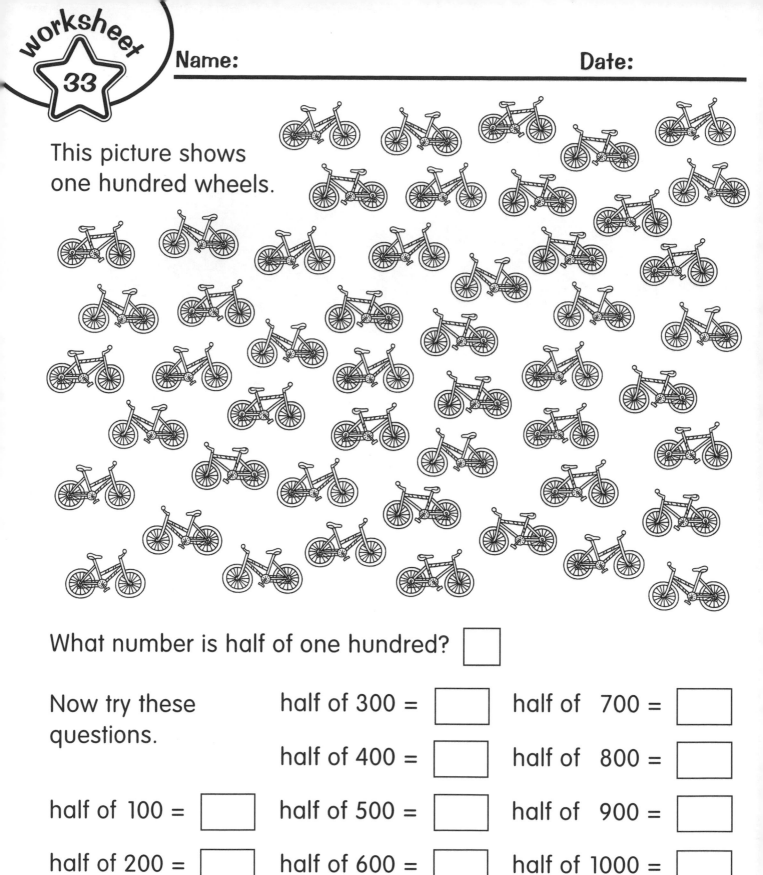

What number is half of one hundred? ☐

Now try these questions.

half of 300 = ☐   half of 700 = ☐

half of 400 = ☐   half of 800 = ☐

half of 100 = ☐   half of 500 = ☐   half of 900 = ☐

half of 200 = ☐   half of 600 = ☐   half of 1000 = ☐

Notes for teachers

Target: Solve one-step problems involving numbers, money or measures, including time; identify patterns or relationships involving numbers; describe and explain methods (Strand 1). Derive and recall multiplication facts and the corresponding division facts; use knowledge of number operations and corresponding inverses, including doubling and halving; identify the doubles of two-digit numbers (Strand 3).

Many children have difficulty halving numbers such as 300 where the hundreds digit is an odd number. Help the child by suggesting s/he splits the 300 into 200 and 100, then to find half of 200 and half of 100 and to combine the two answers. Encourage her/him to use the working out space. Watch carefully how the child does the working out, providing help where necessary. Discuss the answers to the questions with the child. Ask her/him to copy out the answers in a line, in the order of the questions above. Does s/he notice that the answers make a number sequence that goes up in fifties? If so can s/he tell you what half of 1100 is, then half of 1200, etc? Have spare paper ready for the pupil to use for working out.

        Andrew Brodie: Supporting Maths © A & C Black Publishers Ltd. 2007

Name: _____   **Date:** _____

Worksheet
34

Complete the two times table. Copy it out.
Use the multiplication facts to answer the division questions.

1 x 2 = ☐	_____	16 ÷ 2 = ☐
2 x 2 = ☐	_____	10 ÷ 2 = ☐
3 x 2 = ☐	_____	2 ÷ 2 = ☐
4 x 2 = ☐	_____	8 ÷ 2 = ☐
5 x 2 = ☐	_____	18 ÷ 2 = ☐
6 x 2 = ☐	_____	14 ÷ 2 = ☐
7 x 2 = ☐	_____	4 ÷ 2 = ☐
8 x 2 = ☐	_____	20 ÷ 2 = ☐
9 x 2 = ☐	_____	6 ÷ 2 = ☐
10 x 2 = ☐	_____	12 ÷ 2 = ☐

Now try these questions:

50 x 2 = ☐   18 x 2 = ☐   120 x 2 = ☐

100 x 2 = ☐   250 x 2 = ☐   500 x 2 = ☐

25 x 2 = ☐   135 x 2 = ☐

Notes for teachers
Target: Solve one-step problems involving numbers, money or measures, including time; represent the information using numbers or diagrams; make and use tables to organise and interpret information; identify patterns or relationships involving numbers; describe and explain methods (Strand 1). Derive and recall multiplication facts and corresponding division facts; recognise multiples of 2 up to 1000 (Strand 3). Multiply one-digit numbers by 10 (Strand 4).
Once the table is complete discuss any patterns e.g. all the answers are even numbers; the numbers 2, 4, 6, 8 and 0 all appear in the units column twice. Ensure that the child writes out the table as number sentences, i.e. 1 x 2 = 2, etc, so that s/he learns the table as a set of sentences, i.e. 'one times two is two' or 'one two is two, two twos are four', etc. Learning the table off by heart is within the capability of the vast majority of children. A technique that can work well is to ask the child to practise the table by saying it repeatedly for one minute every night for a week. You may like to give the child the 2-times table on Resource sheets A and B (pages 59-60). Encourage the child to say the table in sentences. After the week ask the child to repeat the table to you without looking. Help the child in attempting the questions at the bottom of the sheet. Does s/he notice that these questions are doubles? The working out space should be very useful to the child particularly with questions such as 135 x 2 where s/he could partition the 135 into 100, 30 and 5 before multiplying each part by 2. You could ask the child to complete the multiplications using the 'grid' system – check your school policy on multiplication methods. Have spare paper ready for the pupil to use for working out.

Andrew Brodie: Supporting Maths © A & C Black Publishers Ltd. 2007

Name: _____   **Date:** _____

Complete the three times table. Copy it out.
Use the multiplication facts to answer the division questions.

1 x 3 = ☐	_____	27 ÷ 3 = ☐
2 x 3 = ☐	_____	12 ÷ 3 = ☐
3 x 3 = ☐	_____	9 ÷ 3 = ☐
4 x 3 = ☐	_____	24 ÷ 3 = ☐
5 x 3 = ☐	_____	15 ÷ 3 = ☐
6 x 3 = ☐	_____	6 ÷ 3 = ☐
7 x 3 = ☐	_____	18 ÷ 3 = ☐
8 x 3 = ☐	_____	21 ÷ 3 = ☐
9 x 3 = ☐	_____	3 ÷ 3 = ☐
10 x 3 = ☐	_____	30 ÷ 3 = ☐

Now try these:

21 x 3 = ☐	14 x 3 = ☐	50 x 3 = ☐
25 x 3 = ☐	30 x 3 = ☐	200 x 3 = ☐
100 x 3 = ☐	250 x 3 = ☐	

Notes for teachers

Target: Solve one-step problems involving numbers, money or measures, including time; represent the information using numbers or diagrams; make and use tables to organise and interpret information; identify patterns or relationships involving numbers; describe and explain methods (Strand 1). Derive and recall multiplication facts and corresponding division facts (Strand 3). Multiply one-digit numbers by 10 (Strand 4).

Once the table is complete discuss any patterns: for example, the answers alternate between odd and even numbers. Make sure that the child writes out the table as number sentences, i.e. 1 x 3 = 3, etc, so that s/he learns the table as a set of sentences, i.e. 'one times three is three' or 'one three is three, two threes are six', etc. Learning the table off by heart is within the capability of the vast majority of children. A technique that can work well is to ask the child to practise the table by saying it repeatedly for one minute every night for a week. You may like to give the child a 3-times table card created from Resource sheets A and B (pages 59-60). Encourage the child to say the table in sentences. After the week ask the child to repeat the table to you without looking. Help the child have a go at the questions at the bottom of the page. You could ask the child to complete some of the multiplications using a 'grid' system (check your school policy on multiplication methods) or you may prefer to encourage the child to work out her/his own logical system e.g. for 21 x 3, s/he could do 10 x 3 twice then add 1 x 3. Have spare paper ready for the pupil to use for working out.

Complete the four times table. Copy it out.
Use the multiplication facts to answer the division questions.

1 x 4 = ☐	_____	24 ÷ 4 = ☐
2 x 4 = ☐	_____	16 ÷ 4 = ☐
3 x 4 = ☐	_____	28 ÷ 4 = ☐
4 x 4 = ☐	_____	8 ÷ 4 = ☐
5 x 4 = ☐	_____	20 ÷ 4 = ☐
6 x 4 = ☐	_____	12 ÷ 4 = ☐
7 x 4 = ☐	_____	32 ÷ 4 = ☐
8 x 4 = ☐	_____	40 ÷ 4 = ☐
9 x 4 = ☐	_____	4 ÷ 4 = ☐
10 x 4 = ☐	_____	36 ÷ 4 = ☐

Now try these questions:

20 x 4 = ☐   30 x 4 = ☐   50 x 4 = ☐

100 x 4 = ☐   42 x 4 = ☐   100 ÷ 4 = ☐

25 x 4 = ☐   250 x 4 = ☐

Notes for teachers:
Target: Solve one-step problems involving numbers, money or measures, including time; represent the information using numbers or diagrams; make and use tables to organise and interpret information; identify patterns or relationships involving numbers; describe and explain methods (Strand 1). Derive and recall multiplication facts and corresponding division facts; recognise multiples of 2 up to 1000 (Strand 3). Multiply one-digit numbers by 10 (Strand 4).
Once the table is complete discuss any patterns, for example, the answers are all even numbers and are therefore also multiples of two. Make sure that the child writes out the table as number sentences, i.e. 1 x 4 = 4, etc, so that s/he learns the table as a set of sentences, i.e. 'one times four is four' or 'one four is four, two fours are eight', etc.
Learning the table off by heart is within the capability of the vast majority of children. A technique that can work well is to ask the child to practise the table by saying it repeatedly for one minute every night for a week. You may like to give the child a 4-times table card created from Resource sheets A and B (pages 59-60). Encourage the child to say the table in sentences. After the week ask the child to repeat the table to you without looking. Help the child to have a go at the questions at the bottom of the page. You could ask the child to complete some of the multiplications using a 'grid' system (check your school policy on multiplication methods) or you may prefer to encourage the child to work out her/his own logical system e.g. for 42 x 4, s/he could do 40 x 4 then add 2 x 4. Have spare paper ready for the pupil to use for working out.

Name: _____ **Date:** _____

Complete the five times table. Copy it out.
Use the multiplication facts to answer the division questions.

1 x 5 = ☐	_____	50 ÷ 5 = ☐
2 x 5 = ☐	_____	15 ÷ 5 = ☐
3 x 5 = ☐	_____	30 ÷ 5 = ☐
4 x 5 = ☐	_____	45 ÷ 5 = ☐
5 x 5 = ☐	_____	20 ÷ 5 = ☐
6 x 5 = ☐	_____	10 ÷ 5 = ☐
7 x 5 = ☐	_____	5 ÷ 5 = ☐
8 x 5 = ☐	_____	40 ÷ 5 = ☐
9 x 5 = ☐	_____	25 ÷ 5 = ☐
10 x 5 = ☐	_____	35 ÷ 5 = ☐

Now try these:

100 x 5 = ☐   16 x 5 = ☐   15 x 5 = ☐

50 x 5 = ☐   40 x 5 = ☐   100 ÷ 5 = ☐

25 x 5 = ☐   13 x 5 = ☐

Notes for teachers
Target: Solve one-step problems involving numbers, money or measures, including time; represent the information using numbers or diagrams; make and use tables to organise and interpret information; identify patterns or relationships involving numbers; describe and explain methods. Derive and recall multiplication facts and corresponding division facts; recognise multiples of 5 up to 1000 (Strand 3). Multiply one-digit numbers by 10 (Strand 4).
Make sure that the child writes out the table as number sentences, i.e. 1 x 5 = 5, etc, so that s/he learns the table as a set of sentences, i.e. 'one times five is five' or 'one five is five, two fives are ten', etc. Learning the table off by heart is within the capability of the vast majority of children. A technique that can work well is to ask the child to practise the table by saying it repeatedly for one minute every night for a week. You may like to give the child a 5-times table card created from Resource sheets A and B (pages 59-60). Encourage the child to say the table in sentences. After the week ask the child to repeat the table to you without looking. Help the child have a go at the questions at the bottom of the page. You could ask the child to complete some of the multiplications using a 'grid' system (check your school policy on multiplication methods) or you may prefer to encourage the child to work out her/his own logical system e.g. for 16 x 5, s/he could do 10 x 5 then add 6 x 5. The child may identify the fact that the five times table is special because there is always a five or a zero in the units column. You could extend the activity by showing the child numbers such as 650, which must be a multiple of five because it ends in a zero. Have spare paper ready for the pupil to use for working out.

Andrew Brodie: Supporting Maths © A & C Black Publishers Ltd. 2007

Complete the six times table. Copy it out.
Use the multiplication facts to answer the division questions.

1 x 6 = ☐	_____	6 ÷ 6 = ☐
2 x 6 = ☐	_____	12 ÷ 6 = ☐
3 x 6 = ☐	_____	30 ÷ 6 = ☐
4 x 6 = ☐	_____	48 ÷ 6 = ☐
5 x 6 = ☐	_____	18 ÷ 6 = ☐
6 x 6 = ☐	_____	24 ÷ 6 = ☐
7 x 6 = ☐	_____	36 ÷ 6 = ☐
8 x 6 = ☐	_____	42 ÷ 6 = ☐
9 x 6 = ☐	_____	60 ÷ 6 = ☐
10 x 6 = ☐	_____	54 ÷ 6 = ☐

Now try these:

12 x 6 = ☐   14 x 6 = ☐   25 x 6 = ☐

15 x 6 = ☐   50 x 6 = ☐   16 x 6 = ☐

20 x 6 = ☐   100 x 6 = ☐

Notes for teachers

Target: Solve one-step problems involving numbers, money or measures, including time; represent the information using numbers or diagrams; make and use tables to organise and interpret information; identify patterns or relationships involving numbers; describe and explain methods (Strand 1). Derive and recall multiplication facts and corresponding division facts (Strand 3). Multiply one-digit numbers by 10 (Strand 4).

Once the table is complete discuss any patterns. Make sure that the child writes out the table as number sentences, i.e. 1 x 6 = 6, etc, so that s/he learns the table as a set of sentences, i.e. 'one times six is six' or 'one six is six, two sixes are twelve', etc. Learning the table off by heart is within the capability of the vast majority of children. A technique that can work well is to ask the child to practise the table by saying it repeatedly for one minute every night for a week. You may like to give the child a 6-times table card created from Resource sheets A and B (pages 59-60) at the back of this book. Encourage the child to say the table in sentences. After the week ask the child to repeat the table to you without looking. Help the child to have a go at the questions at the bottom of the page. You could ask the child to complete some of the multiplications using a 'grid' system (check your school policy on multiplication methods) or you may prefer to encourage the child to work out her/his own logical system e.g. for 25 x 6, s/he could do 10 x 6 twice then add 5 x 6. Have spare paper ready for the pupil to use for working out.

Name: _____ **Date:** _____

Complete the seven times table. Copy it out.

Use the multiplication facts to answer the division questions.

1 x 7 = ☐	_____	56 ÷ 7 = ☐
2 x 7 = ☐	_____	28 ÷ 7 = ☐
3 x 7 = ☐	_____	7 ÷ 7 = ☐
4 x 7 = ☐	_____	42 ÷ 7 = ☐
5 x 7 = ☐	_____	14 ÷ 7 = ☐
6 x 7 = ☐	_____	63 ÷ 7 = ☐
7 x 7 = ☐	_____	70 ÷ 7 = ☐
8 x 7 = ☐	_____	49 ÷ 7 = ☐
9 x 7 = ☐	_____	21 ÷ 7 = ☐
10 x 7 = ☐	_____	35 ÷ 7 = ☐

Now try these:

11 x 7 = ☐   20 x 7 = ☐   14 x 7 = ☐

12 x 7 = ☐   21 x 7 = ☐   100 x 7 = ☐

13 x 7 = ☐   30 x 7 = ☐

Notes for teachers

Target: Solve one-step problems involving numbers, money or measures, including time; represent the information using numbers or diagrams; make and use tables to organise and interpret information; identify patterns or relationships involving numbers; describe and explain methods (Strand 1). Derive and recall multiplication facts and corresponding division facts (Strand 3). Multiply one-digit numbers by 10 (Strand 4).

Once the table is complete discuss any patterns, such as odd and even answers. Ensure that the child writes out the table as number sentences, i.e. 1 x 7 = 7, etc, so that s/he learns the table as a set of sentences, i.e. 'one times seven is seven' or 'one seven is seven, two sevens are fourteen', etc. Learning the table off by heart is within the capability of the vast majority of children. A technique that can work well is to ask the child to practise the table by saying it repeatedly for one minute every night for a week. You may like to give the child a 7-times table card created from Resource sheets A and B (pages 59-60). Encourage the child to say the table in sentences. After the week ask the child to repeat the table to you without looking. Help the child to have a go at the questions at the lower part of the page. You could ask the child to complete some of the multiplications using a 'grid' system (check your school policy on multiplication methods) or you may prefer to encourage the child to work out her/his own logical system: the questions given can be worked out from answers that the child already has. Have spare paper ready for the pupil to use for working out.

 Andrew Brodie: Supporting Maths © A & C Black Publishers Ltd. 2007

Name: _____ **Date:** _____

Complete the eight times table. Copy it out.
Use the multiplication facts to answer the division questions.

1 x 8 = ☐ _____ 16 ÷ 8 = ☐

2 x 8 = ☐ _____ 32 ÷ 8 = ☐

3 x 8 = ☐ _____ 80 ÷ 8 = ☐

4 x 8 = ☐ _____ 48 ÷ 8 = ☐

5 x 8 = ☐ _____ 24 ÷ 8 = ☐

6 x 8 = ☐ _____ 64 ÷ 8 = ☐

7 x 8 = ☐ _____ 40 ÷ 8 = ☐

8 x 8 = ☐ _____ 8 ÷ 8 = ☐

9 x 8 = ☐ _____ 56 ÷ 8 = ☐

10 x 8 = ☐ _____ 72 ÷ 8 = ☐

Now try these:

11 x 8 = ☐   20 x 8 = ☐   14 x 8 = ☐

12 x 8 = ☐   25 x 8 = ☐   100 x 8 = ☐

13 x 8 = ☐   30 x 8 = ☐

Notes for teachers

Target: Solve one-step problems involving numbers, money or measures, including time; represent the information using numbers or diagrams; make and use tables to organise and interpret information; identify patterns or relationships involving numbers; describe and explain methods (Strand 1). Derive and recall multiplication facts and corresponding division facts (Strand 3). Multiply one-digit numbers by 10 (Strand 4).

Once the table is complete discuss any patterns, such as the fact that all the answers are even numbers and that the units digit of the answers follows the sequence 8, 6, 4, 2, 0... Make sure that the child writes out the table as number sentences, i.e. 1 x 8 = 8, etc, so that s/he learns the table as a set of sentences, i.e. 'one times eight is eight' or 'one eight is eight, two eights are sixteen', etc. Learning the table off by heart is within the capability of the vast majority of children. A technique that can work well is to ask the child to practise the table by saying it repeatedly for one minute every night for a week. You could give the child an 8-times table card created from Resource sheets A and B (pages 59-60). Encourage the child to say the table in sentences. After the week ask the child to repeat the table to you without looking. Help the child to have a go at the questions at the bottom of the page. You could ask the child to complete some of the multiplications using a 'grid' system (check your school policy on multiplication methods) or you may prefer to encourage the child to work out her/his own logical system: the questions given can be worked out from answers that the child already has. Have spare paper ready for the pupil to use for working out.

Name: _____ **Date:** _____

Complete the nine times table. Copy it out.
Use the multiplication facts to answer the division questions.

1 x 9 = ☐	_____	72 ÷ 9 = ☐
2 x 9 = ☐	_____	36 ÷ 9 = ☐
3 x 9 = ☐	_____	18 ÷ 9 = ☐
4 x 9 = ☐	_____	90 ÷ 9 = ☐
5 x 9 = ☐	_____	9 ÷ 9 = ☐
6 x 9 = ☐	_____	63 ÷ 9 = ☐
7 x 9 = ☐	_____	27 ÷ 9 = ☐
8 x 9 = ☐	_____	45 ÷ 9 = ☐
9 x 9 = ☐	_____	54 ÷ 9 = ☐
10 x 9 = ☐	_____	81 ÷ 9 = ☐

Now try these questions:

11 x 9 = ☐	20 x 9 = ☐	14 x 9 = ☐
12 x 9 = ☐	25 x 9 = ☐	100 x 9 = ☐
13 x 9 = ☐	30 x 9 = ☐	

Notes for teachers

Target: Solve one-step problems involving numbers, money or measures, including time; represent the information using numbers or diagrams; make and use tables to organise and interpret information; identify patterns or relationships involving numbers; describe and explain methods (Strand 1). Derive and recall multiplication facts and corresponding division facts (Strand 3). Multiply one-digit numbers by 10 (Strand 4).

Once the table is complete discuss any patterns. Ask the child to look at the digits in the units column for the whole table, then to look at the digits in the tens column. Ask her/him to add together the two digits for each answer to find interesting results. Make sure that the child writes out the table as number sentences, i.e. 1 x 9 = 9, etc, so that s/he learns the table as a set of sentences, i.e. 'one times nine is nine' or 'one nine is nine, two nines are eighteen', etc. Learning the table off by heart is within the capability of the vast majority of children. A technique that can work well is to ask the child to practise the table by saying it repeatedly for one minute every night for a week. You may like to give the child a 9-times table card created from Resource sheets A and B (pages 59-60). Encourage the child to say the table in sentences. After the week ask the child to repeat the table to you without looking. Help the child to have a go at the questions at the bottom of the page. You could ask the child to complete some of the multiplications using a 'grid' system (check your school policy on multiplication methods) or you may prefer to encourage the child to work out her/his own logical system: the questions given can be worked out from answers that the child already has. Have spare paper ready for the pupil to use for working out.

Andrew Brodie: Supporting Maths © A & C Black Publishers Ltd. 2007

Complete the ten times table. Copy it out.
Use the multiplication facts to answer the division questions.

1 x 10 = ☐	——————————	90 ÷ 10 = ☐
2 x 10 = ☐	——————————	40 ÷ 10 = ☐
3 x 10 = ☐	——————————	70 ÷ 10 = ☐
4 x 10 = ☐	——————————	100 ÷ 10 = ☐
5 x 10 = ☐	——————————	80 ÷ 10 = ☐
6 x 10 = ☐	——————————	20 ÷ 10 = ☐
7 x 10 = ☐	——————————	50 ÷ 10 = ☐
8 x 10 = ☐	——————————	10 ÷ 10 = ☐
9 x 10 = ☐	——————————	60 ÷ 10 = ☐
10 x 10 = ☐	——————————	30 ÷ 10 = ☐

Now try these questions:

11 x 10 = ☐	43 x 10 = ☐	21 x 10 = ☐
12 x 10 = ☐	99 x 10 = ☐	100 x 10 = ☐
20 x 10 = ☐	25 x 10 = ☐	

Notes for teachers
Target: Solve one-step problems involving numbers, money or measures, including time; represent the information using numbers or diagrams; make and use tables to organise and interpret information; identify patterns or relationships involving numbers; describe and explain methods (Strand 1). Derive and recall multiplication facts and corresponding division facts (Strand 3). Multiply one-digit numbers by 10 (Strand 4).
Once the table is complete discuss any patterns, for example, all the answers are even numbers and end in zero. The child may identify the fact that the ten times table is special because there is always a zero in the units column. Before completing the questions at the bottom of the page give the child the opportunity to practise multiplying any two-digit number by ten and observing the effect. S/he could use a calculator to multiply numbers such as 38 by 10. They should be able to see that the 3 digit has moved from the tens column to the hundreds column, the 8 digit has moved from the units column to the tens column and the units column now has a 0. Try to discourage the child from saying 'you just add a nought'. You could give the child a 10-times table card created from Resource sheets A and B (pages 59-60). Most children find the 10-times table the easiest table of all to learn. Encourage the child to say the table in sentences. Have spare paper ready for the pupil to use for working out.

Name: _____ Date: _____

Look at each picture. Under each picture write the decimal number that shows how much is shaded.

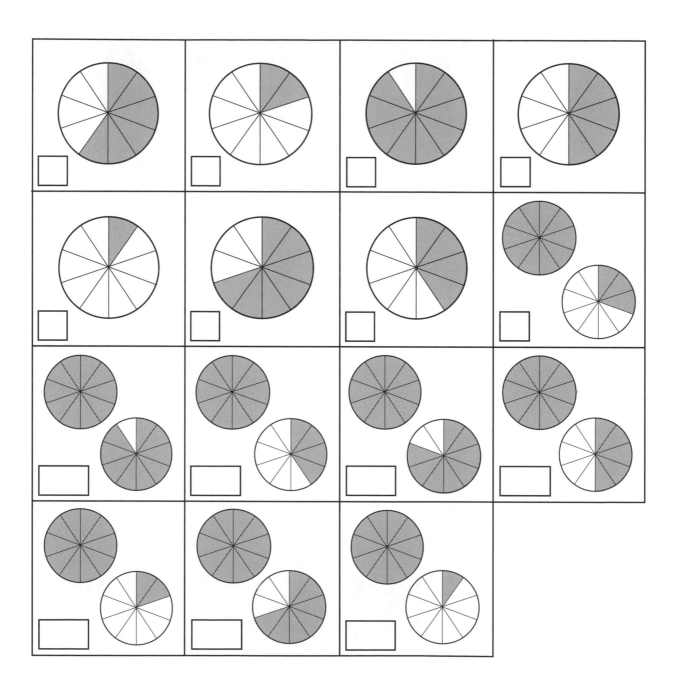

Notes for teachers

Target: Strand 1: identify and use patterns, relationships and properties of numbers.
Strand 2: use decimal notation for tenths; recognise the equivalence between decimal and fraction forms of one half and of tenths.
Discuss the first picture with the child, ensuring that s/he recognises that the 'cake' has been cut into ten equal pieces and encouraging her/him to describe these as tenths. There are six tenths shaded. Show her/him the fraction six tenths ($\frac{6}{10}$). Remind her/him that the bottom of the fraction is called the denominator and shows how many pieces the cake has been cut into and that the top is called the numerator and shows how many pieces we are interested in. Explain that the fraction can be shown as a decimal and that we write this like this: 0·6. Help her/him to complete the first eight questions. Then discuss the picture that shows 1·3 and explain that this can be shown as a mixed number i.e. a whole number and a fraction, one and three tenths ($1\frac{3}{10}$), and that it can be shown as a decimal: 1·3. Help her/him complete the remaining questions. As a final activity ask her/him to identify which picture shows half of a 'cake' shaded. Can s/he write this as a fraction in two different ways and as a decimal?

This number is thirty-six point two: 36.2

This is a decimal point

Match the numbers. The first one has been done for you.

three point four	23.6
seven point nine	78.4
twenty-three point six	3.4
eighteen point two	139.8
thirty-two point six	7.9
seventy-eight point four	18.2
one hundred and thirty-nine point eight	32.6

Listen to your teacher. Write the numbers.

Which of these numbers does the picture show? [   ]

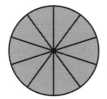 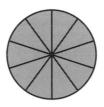 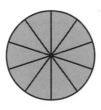  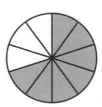

Name: **Date:**

This number is eighteen point three five: **18.35**

This is a decimal point

Match the numbers. The first one has been done for you.

twenty-six point four seven	73.52
eight point three nine	26.47
forty point zero two	40.02
seventeen point nine six	11.28
eleven point two eight	8.39
seventy-three point five two	39.74
thirty-nine point seven four	17.96

Listen to your teacher. Write the numbers.

How much money is shown here?   £ __ . __

Notes for teachers

Target: Identify patterns and relationships involving numbers (Strand 1). Read, write and order whole numbers to at least 1000; use decimal notation for tenths and hundredths; recognise the equivalence between decimal and fraction forms of one half and of tenths (Strand 2).

You may decide to cut off these teachers' notes so that the child cannot see the numbers that you are going to dictate to her/him. Ask the child to look carefully at the number 18.35, explaining that the 1 is in the tens column, the 8 is in the units column, the 3 is in the tenths column and the 5 is in the hundredths column. S/he may need help in reading the word form of the numbers. Note that the child must read the words correctly, i.e. the first written number is twenty-six point four seven not twenty-six point forty-seven.

When the child is ready, dictate the following numbers to her/him:
19.67   2.03   37.84   8.92   128.46   75.83   10.01   88.95   17.32   60.04
Watch carefully how the child writes each number and correct any misunderstandings.

Andrew Brodie: Supporting Maths © A & C Black Publishers Ltd. 2007

Write the correct fraction or mixed number in each box.

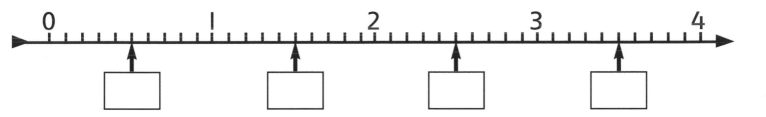

Write the correct decimal number in each box.

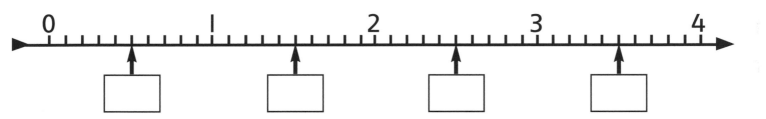

Write the correct decimal number in each box.

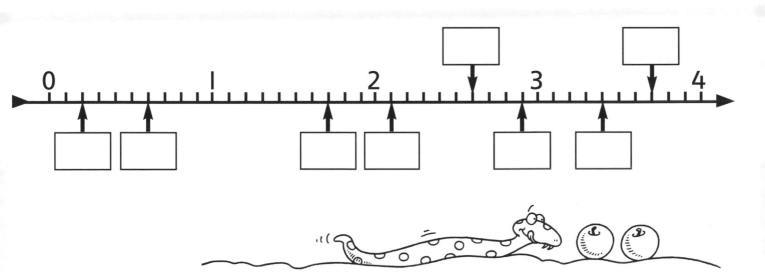

Notes for teachers
Target: Solve one-step problems involving numbers, money or measures, including time; identify patterns or relationships involving numbers; describe and explain methods (Strand 1). Read, write and order whole numbers to at least 1000; use decimal notation for tenths and hundredths; recognise the equivalence between decimal and fraction forms of one half and of tenths; position one-place decimals on a number line; use diagrams to interpret equivalent fractions; interpret mixed numbers and position them on a number line (Strand 2).
Discuss the first number line with the child, reminding her/him that a mixed number is a whole number with a fraction. Help her/him in writing $\frac{1}{2}$, $1\frac{1}{2}$, $2\frac{1}{2}$, $3\frac{1}{2}$ in the correct places. Ask her/him where s/he thinks the fraction one quarter would be on the number line, then three quarters, etc. Ask the child to write the correct decimal numbers in the boxes for the second line: 0.5, 1.5, 2.5 and 3.5. Can s/he see that the two lines are the same? Can s/he recognise that $\frac{1}{2}$ and 0.5 are worth the same i.e. they are equivalent? Discuss and match all the numbers shown. Now ask her/him to complete the third line.

Andrew Brodie: Supporting Maths © A & C Black Publishers Ltd. 2007   51

Name: _____   **Date:** _____

Lee has got 40 pence. He says he will give his sister a quarter of the money if she can tell him what a quarter of 40p is.
Do you know the answer?

$\frac{1}{4}$ of 40p = ☐

Can you find these amounts?

$\frac{1}{3}$ of 30p = ☐ $\frac{1}{4}$ of 20p = ☐ $\frac{1}{3}$ of 60p = ☐

$\frac{1}{5}$ of 50p = ☐ $\frac{1}{2}$ of 40p = ☐ $\frac{1}{4}$ of 80p = ☐

$\frac{1}{2}$ of 50p = ☐ $\frac{1}{6}$ of 24p = ☐ $\frac{3}{4}$ of 40p = ☐

Notes for teachers
Target: Solve one-step problems involving numbers, money or measures, including time; identify patterns or relationships involving numbers; describe and explain methods (Strand 1). Read and write proper fractions interpreting the denominator as the parts of a whole and the numerator as the number of parts; find fractions of numbers, quantities or shapes (Strand 2). Read the fractions with the child and help her/him to understand that s/he is finding a fraction of each amount of money. For the first question (finding a quarter of 40p) dividing 40 by 4 will give the correct answer because the denominator tells us how many parts to split the total into. Many children are able to find quarters easily by halving then halving again but for most of the questions shown, as the amounts are not being quartered, it is more appropriate to use the division method. With the last question take the opportunity to explain that the top of the fraction, the numerator, shows us that we need to keep three of the quarters.

        Andrew Brodie: Supporting Maths © A & C Black Publishers Ltd. 2007

Name: _____   **Date:** _____

Listen to your teacher. Colour the fractions.
Write the fractions.

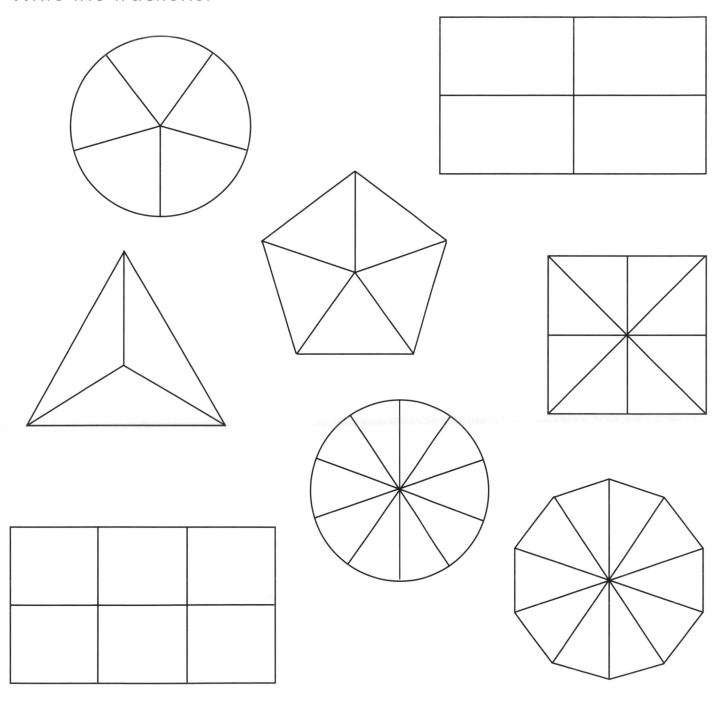

Notes for teachers

Target: Solve one-step problems involving numbers, money or measures, including time; identify patterns or relationships involving numbers; describe and explain methods (Strand 1). Read and write proper fractions interpreting the denominator as the parts of a whole and the numerator as the number of parts; identify and estimate fractions of shapes; use diagrams to compare fractions (Strand 2). Identify pairs of fractions that total 1 (Strand 3).

Help the child colour the shapes as follows: Colour four fifths of the circle; colour three eighths of the square; colour three quarters of the rectangle; colour two thirds of the triangle; colour half of the circle; colour five sixths of the rectangle; colour two fifths of the pentagon; colour seven tenths of the decagon. Ask the child to write the fraction coloured next to each shape. Discuss each shape asking the child what fraction of each is not coloured. Show her/him that $\frac{4}{5} + \frac{1}{5} = 1$ for the first circle (where 1 represents one whole circle). Ask her/him if s/he can write a similar number sentence for each of the other shapes.

Name: _____   **Date:** _____

Use your ruler to measure these lines to the nearest millimetre.
The first two lines have been measured for you.

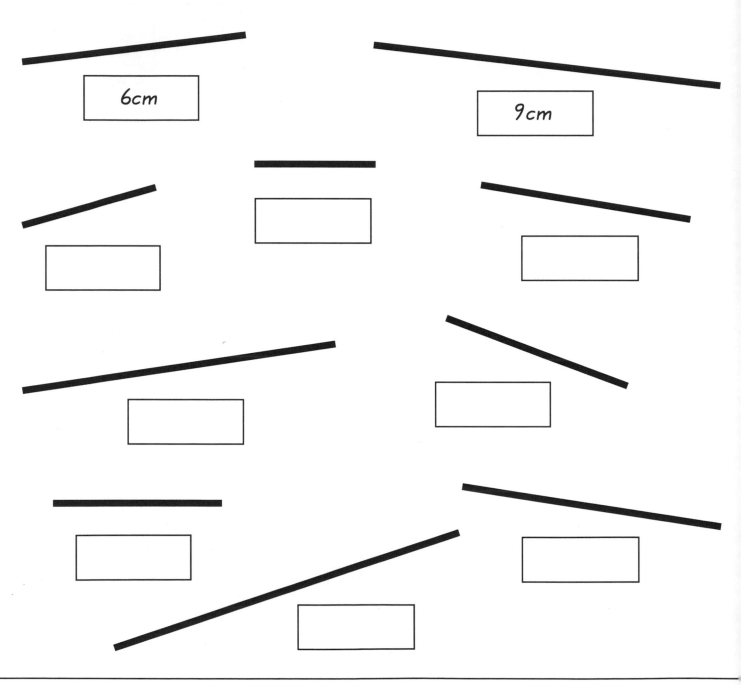

6cm

9cm

Notes for teachers

Target: Solve one-step problems involving numbers, money or measures; follow a line of enquiry by deciding what information is important; describe and explain methods (Strand 1). Read, to the nearest division and half-division, scales that are numbered or partially numbered; use the information to measure and draw to a suitable degree of accuracy; use decimal notation to record measurements (Strand 6).

Examine the child's ruler with her/him, ensuring that s/he can identify the centimetre and millimetre markings. Does s/he know that 1cm = 10mm? Help her/him in stating the number of millimetres for each centimetre marking i.e. 2cm = 20mm, 3cm = 30mm, etc. Help her/him to measure the first line to confirm that it is 6cm long as written on the sheet. Ask her/him what this measurement would be in millimetres. Look at the second line in the same way and point out that the length has been written in centimetres using a decimal point because each millimetre is one tenth of a centimetre. Then ask the child to measure the other lines. Check that s/he is measuring from the zero mark and not from the very end of the ruler and that s/he is writing the measurements down correctly using decimal notation. As an extension activity you could ask the child to draw some lines to lengths that you specify.

Andrew Brodie: Supporting Maths © A & C Black Publishers Ltd. 2007

Name: **Date:**

This is Arnold the Ant.
Find how far Arnold has to walk to get
round each rectangle. This distance is called the perimeter.

3cm   4cm   3cm

8cm

Perimeter =
Area =

8cm

6cm

Perimeter =
Area =

Perimeter =
Area =

Perimeter =
Area =

5cm

Perimeter =
Area =

Perimeter =
Area =

3cm

7cm

6cm

Now count the squares to find out how much space Arnold has
in each rectangle. This space is called the area.

Notes for teachers
Target: Solve one-step problems involving numbers, money or measures, choosing and carrying out appropriate calculations; follow a line of enquiry by deciding what information is important; describe and explain methods (Strand 1). Choose and use standard metric units and their abbreviations when estimating, measuring and recording length; draw rectangles and measure and calculate their perimeters; find the area of rectilinear shapes drawn on a square grid by counting squares (Strand 6).
Ensure that the child understands that perimeter refers to the distance around the rectangle. S/he can find each perimeter by counting centimetres all the way round each shape but s/he could also use addition by e.g. completing 8 + 3 + 8 + 3 for the first shape. Finding the perimeter can be demonstrated by using a ruler and measuring each side instead of counting the edges of the squares. This avoids the situation where a child is counting the squares themselves rather than the edges. Many children confuse perimeter with area. Help them to understand that the area can be found by counting squares to measure the amount of space covered, whereas the perimeter is found by counting the edges of squares to work out the distance around a shape.

Name: Date:

Some points are marked on the grid.

We can describe where each point is by using coordinates.

Point A has coordinates (**7**, **3**) because it matches the number **7** on the **x-axis** and the number **3** on the **y-axis**.

Coordinates are always written in brackets.

The **x** coordinate is always written first.

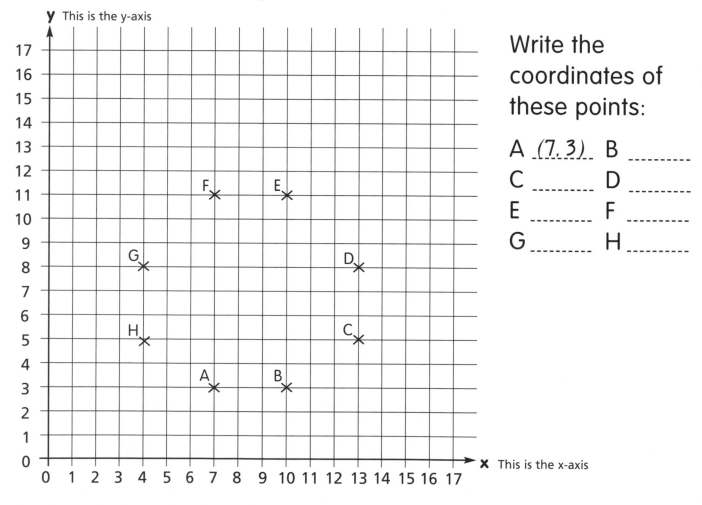

Write the coordinates of these points:

A _(7, 3)_ B _____

C _____ D _____

E _____ F _____

G _____ H _____

Join A to B, B to C, C to D, D to E, E to F, F to G, G to H and H to A by drawing straight lines.

What shape have you drawn? _____

Now draw a square on the grid and write down the coordinates of its corners. _____ _____ _____ _____

Notes for teachers

Target: Solve one-step problems involving numbers, money or measures, choosing and carrying out appropriate calculations; follow a line of enquiry by deciding what information is important; describe and explain methods (Strand 1). Read and plot coordinates in the first quadrant (Strand 5).

Most children find this aspect of maths fairly straightforward provided they know and understand the terminology. The key words are all shown on this worksheet. Discuss the activity with the child ensuring that s/he understands the vocabulary.

Name: _____   **Date:** _____

Read this short piece of writing:

> Yesterday I went shopping. I bought some eggs, a loaf of bread, some cheese and some milk. Just when I reached home I realised that I had forgotten to buy some butter.

We want to find out which letter appears most often.
Draw a tally chart showing how many times each letter of the alphabet appears in the writing.

a		h		o		v	
b		i		p		w	
c		j		q		x	
d		k		r		y	
e		l		s		z	
f		m		t			
g		n		u			

Notes for teachers

Target: Solve one-step problems involving numbers, money or measures, choosing and carrying out appropriate calculations; follow a line of enquiry by deciding what information is important; describe and explain methods; collect, organise and interpret selected information to find answers (Strand 1). Answer a question by identifying what data to collect; organise, present, analyse and interpret the data in tables, tally charts and bar charts (please note that the Framework also lists diagrams and pictograms) (Strand 7).
Help the child in completing the tally. An effective method is to start at the beginning of the writing and to work through it letter by letter rather than starting with the letter a and working through the alphabet. Thus the child should start by crossing out the letter Y in Yesterday and putting a tally mark by the y in the table, then cross out and tally the letter e, etc. Remind the child that every fifth line goes across the previous four in the tally. Once the child has completed the task ask her/him to complete Worksheet 53.

Name: **Date:**

Look again at the writing on Worksheet 52.
We want to find out which letter appears most often. Use your tally chart to complete this bar chart.

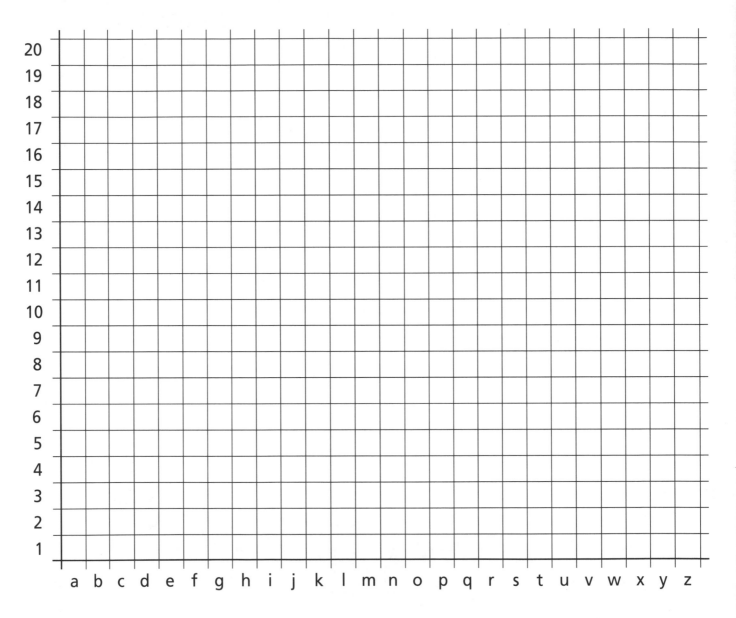

Colour a bar for each letter unless the letter has no tally score.

Notes for teachers
Target: Solve one-step problems involving numbers, money or measures, choosing and carrying out appropriate calculations; follow a line of enquiry by deciding what information is important; describe and explain methods; collect, organise and interpret selected information to find answers (Strand 1). Answer a question by identifying what data to collect; organise, present, analyse and interpret the data in tables, tally charts and bar charts (please note that the Framework also lists diagrams and pictograms) (Strand 7).
Help the child to use her/his tally chart to complete the bar chart. Once the bar chart is coloured discuss the following with the child: Which letter appears most often in this piece of writing? Which letter appears least often in this piece of writing? Which letters do not appear in this piece of writing? How many more times does letter e appear than letter a? Which is the most common consonant in this piece of writing? Do you think we would get the same results with a different piece of writing?

Times Tables

These tables can be photocopied back to back with the written tables shown on Resource sheet B. They can be laminated then cut into separate tables so that the child can take them away to practise.

1 x 2 = 2	1 x 3 = 3	1 x 4 = 4
2 x 2 = 4	2 x 3 = 6	2 x 4 = 8
3 x 2 = 6	3 x 3 = 9	3 x 4 = 12
4 x 2 = 8	4 x 3 = 12	4 x 4 = 16
5 x 2 = 10	5 x 3 = 15	5 x 4 = 20
6 x 2 = 12	6 x 3 = 18	6 x 4 = 24
7 x 2 = 14	7 x 3 = 21	7 x 4 = 28
8 x 2 = 16	8 x 3 = 24	8 x 4 = 32
9 x 2 = 18	9 x 3 = 27	9 x 4 = 36
10 x 2 = 20	10 x 3 = 30	10 x 4 = 40

1 x 5 = 5	1 x 6 = 6	1 x 7 = 7
2 x 5 = 10	2 x 6 = 12	2 x 7 = 14
3 x 5 = 15	3 x 6 = 18	3 x 7 = 21
4 x 5 = 20	4 x 6 = 24	4 x 7 = 28
5 x 5 = 25	5 x 6 = 30	5 x 7 = 35
6 x 5 = 30	6 x 6 = 36	6 x 7 = 42
7 x 5 = 35	7 x 6 = 42	7 x 7 = 49
8 x 5 = 40	8 x 6 = 48	8 x 7 = 56
9 x 5 = 45	9 x 6 = 54	9 x 7 = 63
10 x 5 = 50	10 x 6 = 60	10 x 7 = 70

1 x 8 = 8	1 x 9 = 9	1 x 10 = 10
2 x 8 = 16	2 x 9 = 18	2 x 10 = 20
3 x 8 = 24	3 x 9 = 27	3 x 10 = 30
4 x 8 = 32	4 x 9 = 36	4 x 10 = 40
5 x 8 = 40	5 x 9 = 45	5 x 10 = 50
6 x 8 = 48	6 x 9 = 54	6 x 10 = 60
7 x 8 = 56	7 x 9 = 63	7 x 10 = 70
8 x 8 = 64	8 x 9 = 72	8 x 10 = 80
9 x 8 = 72	9 x 9 = 81	9 x 10 = 90
10 x 8 = 80	10 x 9 = 90	10 x 10 = 100

Resource sheet B

Times tables in words

These tables can be photocopied back to back with the tables shown on Resource sheet A. They can be laminated then cut into separate tables so that the child can take them away to practise.

One four is four	One three is three	One two is two
Two fours are eight	Two threes are six	Two twos are four
Three fours are twelve	Three threes are nine	Three twos are six
Four fours are sixteen	Four threes are twelve	Four twos are eight
Five fours are twenty	Five threes are fifteen	Five twos are ten
Six fours are twenty-four	Six threes are eighteen	Six twos are twelve
Seven fours are twenty-eight	Seven threes are twenty-one	Seven twos are fourteen
Eight fours are thirty-two	Eight threes are twenty-four	Eight twos are sixteen
Nine fours are thirty-six	Nine threes are twenty-seven	Nine twos are eighteen
Ten fours are forty	Ten threes are thirty	Ten twos are twenty

One seven is seven	One six is six	One five is five
Two sevens are fourteen	Two sixes are twelve	Two fives are ten
Three sevens are twenty-one	Three sixes are eighteen	Three fives are fifteen
Four sevens are twenty-eight	Four sixes are twenty-four	Four fives are twenty
Five sevens are thirty-five	Five sixes are thirty	Five fives are twenty-five
Six sevens are forty-two	Six sixes are thirty-six	Six fives are thirty
Seven sevens are forty-nine	Seven sixes are forty-two	Seven fives are thirty-five
Eight sevens are fifty-six	Eight sixes are forty-eight	Eight fives are forty
Nine sevens are sixty-three	Nine sixes are fifty-four	Nine fives are forty-five
Ten sevens are seventy	Ten sixes are sixty	Ten fives are fifty

One ten is ten	One nine is nine	One eight is eight
Two tens are twenty	Two nines are eighteen	Two eights are sixteen
Three tens are thirty	Three nines are twenty-seven	Three eights are twenty-four
Four tens are forty	Four nines are thirty-six	Four eights are thirty-two
Five tens are fifty	Five nines are forty-five	Five eights are forty
Six tens are sixty	Six nines are fifty-four	Six eights are forty-eight
Seven tens are seventy	Seven nines are sixty-three	Seven eights are fifty-six
Eight tens are eighty	Eight nines are seventy-two	Eight eights are sixty-four
Nine tens are ninety	Nine nines are eighty-one	Nine eights are seventy-two
Ten tens are a hundred	Ten nines are ninety	Ten eights are eighty

Andrew Brodie: Supporting Maths © A & C Black Publishers Ltd. 2007

Multiplication square

x	1	2	3	4	5	6	7	8	9	10
1	1	2	3	4	5	6	7	8	9	10
2	2	4	6	8	10	12	14	16	18	20
3	3	6	9	12	15	18	21	24	27	30
4	4	8	12	16	20	24	28	32	36	40
5	5	10	15	20	25	30	35	40	45	50
6	6	12	18	24	30	36	42	48	54	60
7	7	14	21	28	35	42	49	56	63	70
8	8	16	24	32	40	48	56	64	72	80
9	9	18	27	36	45	54	63	72	81	90
10	10	20	30	40	50	60	70	80	90	100

Make your own multiplication square.

x	1	2	3	4	5	6	7	8	9	10
1										
2										
3										
4										
5										
6										
7										
8										
9										
10										

 Andrew Brodie: Supporting Maths © A & C Black Publishers Ltd. 2007

Blank multiplication square

Mini facts

Multiplication tables

x	1	2	3	4	5	6	7	8	9	10
1	1	2	3	4	5	6	7	8	9	10
2	2	4	6	8	10	12	14	16	18	20
3	3	6	9	12	15	18	21	24	27	30
4	4	8	12	16	20	24	28	32	36	40
5	5	10	15	20	25	30	35	40	45	50
6	6	12	18	24	30	36	42	48	54	60
7	7	14	21	28	35	42	49	56	63	70
8	8	16	24	32	40	48	56	64	72	80
9	9	18	27	36	45	54	63	72	81	90
10	10	20	30	40	50	60	70	80	90	100

Measurement facts

1 kilogram = 1000 grams
(1kg = 1000g)

1 kilometre = 1000 metres
(1km = 1000m)

1 metre = 100 centimetres
(1m = 100cm)

1 metre = 1000 millimetres
(1m = 1000mm)

1 litre = 1000 millilitres
(1l = 1000ml)

Angle facts

This is a right angle.
A right angle has 90°.

Two right angles together make a straight line. The straight line has 180° around this point.

This is an acute angle. An acute angle is less than 90°.

This is an obtuse angle. An obtuse angle is more than 90° and less than 180°.

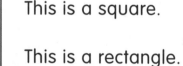
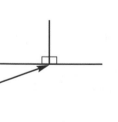
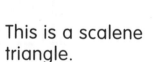

Shapes

This is a square.

This is a rectangle.

This is a scalene triangle.

This is an isosceles triangle.

This is an equilateral triangle.

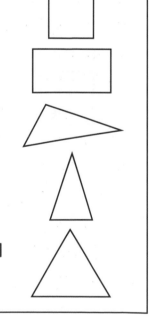